PRAISE FOR *A NATION UNMADE BY WAR*

"Unlike lesser writers distracted by the latest antics of the man with the orange hair, the brilliant Tom Engelhardt keeps our focus where it should be: on the thousands of lives and trillions of dollars we spend in unending wars, on the vast militarized empire whose leaders' belief that they can control the world undermines our children's future and sends young men and women to die in fruitless conflicts."
—Adam Hochschild, author of *Spain in Our Hearts*

"The mainstream media call it the 'Age of Trump.' Tom Engelhardt knows better: it's the 'Era of America Unhinged.' This new collection of essays gives us Engelhardt at his very best: incisive, impassioned, and funny even, in a time of great darkness."
—Andrew Bacevich, author of *America's War for the Greater Middle East*

"Tom Engelhardt is a tireless analyst of the miseries of American Empire. In this indispensable book he shines an unrelenting spotlight on the steep cost to everyday Americans of the sunny fantasies about Middle East dominance retailed by generals, politicians, and think tank rats inside the Beltway—fairy tales intended to obscure the dark failures of this enterprise."
—Juan Cole, author of *The New Arabs*

"We Americans have learned to sleep through our multiple wars, but Tom Engelhardt relentlessly shakes us awake. For sixteen years now, he has watched in astonishment and written the scene-by-scene review of this imploding empire, and he only becomes sharper as old reels rewind and play again. In this volume, the nation wasted at home by its profligate wars abroad picks a big orange emperor, flanked by his very own generals, to lead us on into . . . well, just read the book!"
—Ann Jones, author of *They Were Soldiers*

For Patrick,
Whose support has meant the world
to me — and to TomDispatch...

love
Tom
5/10/18

A
NATION
UNMADE
BY WAR

A TomDispatch Book

TOM ENGELHARDT

Haymarket Books
Chicago, IL

© 2018 Tom Engelhardt

Published in 2018 by
Haymarket Books
P.O. Box 180165
Chicago, IL 60618
773-583-7884
www.haymarketbooks.org
info@haymarketbooks.org

ISBN: 978-1-60846-901-7

Trade distribution:
In the US, Consortium Book Sales and Distribution, www.cbsd.com
In Canada, Publishers Group Canada, www.pgcbooks.ca
In the UK, Turnaround Publisher Services, www.turnaround-uk.com
All other countries, IPS International, IPS_Intlsales@ingramcontent.com

This book was published with the generous support of Lannan Foundation
and Wallace Action Fund.

Cover design by Mimi Bark.

Printed in Canada by union labor.

Library of Congress Cataloging-in-Publication data is available.

10 9 8 7 6 5 4 3 2 1

For Will and Maggie.
My life would be unimaginable without you.

CONTENTS

An Empire of Nothing at All?

As I was taking a last look at this book, the Costs of War Project at Brown University's Watson Institute published a new estimate of the taxpayer dollars that will have gone into America's war on terror from September 12, 2001, through fiscal year 2018. That figure: a cool $5.6 trillion (including the future costs of caring for our war vets). On average, that's at least $23,386 per taxpayer.

Keep in mind that such figures, however eye-popping, are only the dollar costs of our wars. They don't, for instance, include the psychic costs to the Americans mangled in one way or another in those never-ending conflicts. They don't include the costs to this country's infrastructure, which has been crumbling while taxpayer dollars flow copiously and in a remarkably—in these years, almost uniquely—bipartisan fashion into what's still laughably called "national security." That's not, of course, what would make most of *us* more secure, but what would make *them*—the denizens of the national security state—ever more secure in Washington and elsewhere. We're talking about the Pentagon, the Department of Homeland Security, the US nuclear complex, and the rest of that state-within-a-state, including its many intelligence agencies and the warrior corporations that have, by now, been fused into that vast and vastly profitable interlocking structure.

In reality, the costs of America's wars, still spreading in the Trump era, are incalculable. Just look at photos of the cities of Ramadi or Mosul in Iraq, Raqqa or Aleppo in Syria, Sirte in Libya, or Marawi in the southern Philippines, all in ruins in the wake of the conflicts Washington set off in the post–9/11 years, and try to put a price on them. Those views of mile upon mile of rubble, often without a building still standing untouched, should take anyone's breath away. Some of those cities may never be fully rebuilt.

And how could you even begin to put a dollars-and-cents value on the larger human costs of those wars: the hundreds of thousands of dead? The tens of millions of people displaced in their own countries or sent as refugees fleeing across any border in sight? How could you factor in the way those masses of uprooted peoples of the Greater Middle East and Africa are unsettling other parts of the planet? Their presence (or more accurately a growing fear of it) has, for instance, helped fuel an expanding set of right-wing "populist" movements that threaten to tear Europe apart. And who could forget the role that those refugees—or at least fantasy versions of them—played in Donald Trump's full-throated, successful pitch for the presidency? What, in the end, might be the cost of that?

Opening the Gates of Hell

America's never-ending twenty-first-century conflicts were triggered by the decision of George W. Bush and his top officials to instantly define their response to attacks on the Pentagon and the World Trade Center by a tiny group of jihadis as a "war"; then to proclaim it nothing short of a "Global War on Terror"; and finally to invade and occupy first Afghanistan and then Iraq, with dreams of dominating the Greater Middle East—and ultimately the planet—as no other imperial power had ever done.

Their overwrought geopolitical fantasies and their sense that the US military was a force capable of accomplishing anything they willed it to do launched a process that would cost this world of ours in ways that no one will ever be able to calculate. Who, for instance, could begin to put a price on the futures of the children whose lives, in the aftermath of those decisions, would be twisted and shrunk in ways frightening even to imagine? Who could tote up what it means for so many millions of this planet's young to be deprived of homes, parents, educations—of anything, in fact, approximating the sort of stability that might lead to a future worth imagining?

Though few may remember it, I've never forgotten the 2002 warning issued by Amr Moussa, then head of the Arab League. An invasion of Iraq would, he predicted that September, "open the gates of hell." Two years later, in the wake of the actual invasion and the US occupation of that country, he altered his comment slightly. "The gates of hell," he said, "are open in Iraq."

His assessment has proven unbearably prescient—and one not only applicable to Iraq. Fourteen years after that invasion, we should all now be in some kind of mourning for a world that won't ever be. It wasn't just the US military that, in the spring of 2003, passed through those gates to hell. In our own way, we all did. Otherwise, Donald Trump wouldn't have become president.

I don't claim to be an expert on hell. I have no idea exactly what circle of it we're now in, but I do know one thing: we are there.

The Infrastructure of a Garrison State

If I could bring my parents back from the dead right now, I know that this country in its present state would boggle their minds. They wouldn't recognize it. If I were to tell them, for instance, that just three men—Bill Gates, Jeff Bezos, and Warren Buffett—now possess as much wealth as the bottom half of the US population, of 160 million Americans, they would never believe me.

How, for instance, could I begin to explain to them the ways in which, in these years, money flowed ever upward into the pockets of the immensely wealthy and then down again into what became one-percent elections that would finally ensconce a billionaire and his family in the White House? How would I explain to them that, while leading congressional Democrats and Republicans couldn't say often enough that this country was uniquely greater than any that ever existed, none of them could find the funds—some $5.6 trillion for starters—necessary for our roads, dams, bridges, tunnels, and other crucial infrastructure? This on a planet where what the news likes to call "extreme weather" is increasingly wreaking havoc on that same infrastructure.

My parents wouldn't have thought such things possible. Not in America. And somehow I'd have to explain to them that they had returned to a nation which, though few Americans realize it, has increasingly been unmade by war—by the conflicts Washington's war on terror triggered that have now morphed into the wars of so many and have, in the process, changed us.

Such conflicts on the global frontiers have a tendency to come home in ways that can be hard to track or pin down. After all, unlike those cities in the Greater Middle East, ours aren't yet in ruins—though some of them may be heading in that direction, even if in slow motion. This country is, at least theoretically, still near the height of its imperial power, still the wealthiest nation on the planet. And yet it should be clear enough by now that we've crippled not just other nations but ourselves in ways that I suspect—though I've tried over these years to absorb and record them as best I could—we can still barely see or grasp.

In this book, selected and edited from my commentaries at *Tom-Dispatch* since 2016, the focus is on a nation increasingly unsettled and transformed by spreading wars to which most of its citizens were, at best, only half paying attention. Certainly, Trump's election was a sign of how an American sense of decline had already come home to roost in the era of the rise of the national security state (and little else).

Though it's not something normally said here, to my mind President Trump should be considered part of the costs of those wars come home. Without the invasions of Afghanistan and Iraq and what followed, I doubt he would have been imaginable as anything but the host of a reality TV show or the owner of a series of failed casinos. Nor would the garrison-state version of Washington he now occupies be conceivable, nor the generals of our disastrous wars whom he's surrounded himself with, nor the growth of a surveillance state that would have staggered George Orwell.

The Makings of a Blowback Machine

It took Donald Trump—give him credit where it's due—to make us begin to grasp that we were living in a different and devolving world. And none of this would have been imaginable if, in the aftermath of 9/11, George W. Bush, Dick Cheney & Co. hadn't felt the urge to launch the wars that led us through those gates of hell. Their soaring geopolitical dreams of global domination proved to be nightmares of the first order. They imagined a planet unlike any in the previous half millennium of imperial history, in which a single power would basically dominate everything until the end of time. They imagined, that is, the sort of world that, in Hollywood, had been associated only with the most malign of evil characters.

And here was the result of their conceptual overreach: never, it could be argued, has a great power still in its imperial prime proven quite so incapable of applying its military and political might in a way that would advance its aims. It's a strange fact of this century that the US military has been deployed across vast swaths of the planet and somehow, again and again, has found itself overmatched by underwhelming enemy forces and incapable of producing any results other than destruction and further fragmentation. And all of this occurred at the moment when the planet most needed a new kind of knitting together, at the moment when humanity's future was at stake in ways previously unimaginable, thanks to its still-increasing use of fossil fuels.

In the end, the last empire may prove to be an empire of nothing at all—a grim possibility which has been a focus of *TomDispatch*, the website I've run since November 2002. Of course, when you write pieces for such a website every couple of weeks for years on end, it would be surprising if you didn't repeat yourself (something I've done my best to keep to a minimum in the text that follows). The real repetitiousness, however, wasn't at *TomDispatch*. It was in Washington. The only thing our leaders and generals have seemed capable of doing, starting from the day after the 9/11 attacks, is more or less the same thing with the same dismal results, again and again.

The US military and the national security state that those wars em-
boldened have become, in effect—and with a bow to the late Chalmers
Johnson (a *TomDispatch* stalwart and a man who knew the gates of hell
when he saw them)—a staggeringly well-funded blowback machine.
In all these years, while three administrations pursued the spreading
war on terror, America's conflicts in distant lands were largely after-
thoughts to its citizenry. Despite the largest demonstrations in history
aimed at stopping a war before it began, once the invasion of Iraq occurred, the protests died out and, ever since, Americans have generally
ignored their country's wars, even as the blowback began. Someday,
they will have no choice but to pay attention.

ONE

Where Did the American Century Go?

Vladimir Putin admitted it: the United States remains the planet's sole superpower, as it has been since the Soviet Union collapsed in 1991. "America," the Russian president said in June 2016, "is a great power. Today, probably the only superpower. We accept that."

The United States is the default superpower in an ever-more recalcitrant world.

Seventy-five years ago, at the edge of a global conflagration among rival great powers and empires, Henry Luce first suggested that the next century could be ours. In February 1941, in his magazine, *LIFE*, he wrote a famous essay entitled "The American Century." In it, he proclaimed that if only Americans would think internationally, surge into the world, and accept that they were already at war, the next hundred years would be theirs. Just over nine months later, the Japanese attacked the US fleet at Pearl Harbor, plunging the country into World War II. At the time, however, Americans were still riven and confused about how to deal with spreading regional conflicts in Europe and Asia, as well as the rise of fascism and the Nazis.

That moment was a horrific one, and yet it was also just a heightened version of what had gone before. For the previous half millennium, there had seldom been a moment when at least two (and often three or more) European powers had not been in contention, often armed and violent, for domination and for control of significant parts of the planet. Over those many centuries, great powers rose and fell and new ones, including Germany and Japan, came on the scene, girded for imperial battle. In the process, a modern global arms race was launched to create ever-more advanced and devastating weaponry based on the latest breakthroughs in the science of war. By August 1945, this had led to the release of an awesome form of primal energy in the first (and so far, only) use of nuclear weapons in wartime.

In the years that followed, the United States and the Soviet Union grew ever more "super" and took possession of destructive capabilities once left, at least in the human imagination, to the gods: the power to annihilate not just one enemy on one battlefield or one armada on one sea, but everything. In the nearly half century of the Cold War, the rivalry between them became apocalyptic in nature as their nuclear arsenals grew to monstrous proportions. As a result, with the exception of the Cuban Missile Crisis, they faced off against each other indirectly in "limited" proxy wars that, especially in Korea and Indochina, were of unparalleled technological ferocity.

Then, in 1991, the Soviet Union imploded, and for the first time in historical memory, there was only one power that mattered. This was a reality even Henry Luce might have found far-fetched. Previously, the idea of a single power so mighty that it alone loomed over the planet was essentially relegated to fictional fantasies about extraordinary evil. And yet, so it was—or at least so it seemed, especially to the leadership that took power in Washington in the year 2000 and soon enough were dreaming of a planetary *Pax Americana*.

In a strange way, something similarly unimaginable happened in Europe. On that continent laid waste by two devastating twentieth-century wars, a single "union" was formed, something that not so long before would have been categorized as a madly utopian project. The idea that centuries of national rivalries and the rabid nationalism that often went with them could somehow be tamed and that former great powers and imperial contenders could be subsumed in a single peaceful organization (even if under the aegis of American global power) would once have seemed like the most absurd of fictions. And yet so it would be—or so it seemed, at least until recently.

A Planetary Brexit?

We seldom take in the strangeness of what's happened on this curious planet of ours. In the years after 1991, we became so inured to the idea of a single-superpower globe and a single European economic and political union that both, once utterly inconceivable, came to seem too mundane to spend a lot of time thinking about. And yet, who would have believed that seventy-five years after Luce urged his country into that American Century, there would, in military terms, be no genuine rivals, no other truly great global powers (only regional ones) on Planet Earth?

So many taken-for-granted things about our world were considered utterly improbable before they happened. Take China. I recall well the day in 1972 when, after decades of non-contact and raging hostility, we learned that President Richard Nixon and his national security advisor, Henry Kissinger, were in Beijing meeting congenially with Communist leader Mao Zedong. When a friend called to tell me the news, I thought he was joking and it struck me as a ridiculously lame joke at that.

There's almost no way now to capture how improbable this seemed at the time—the leading Communist revolutionary on the planet chatting cheerily with the prime representative of anti-communism. If, however, you had told me then that in the decades to come China would undergo a full-scale capitalist revolution and become the economic powerhouse of the planet, and that this would be done under the leadership of Mao's still-regnant Communist Party, I would have considered you mad.

And that's just to begin to mention the implausibilities of the present moment. After all, in what fantasies—ever—of a globe with a single dominant power, was it imagined that this power would fail so utterly to bring the world to anything approximating heel? If you had told Henry Luce, or anyone else, including the future masters of the universe in Washington in 1991, that the only superpower left on

Earth, with the best-funded, mightiest, most technologically destructive and advanced military would, on September 11, 2001, be goaded by a group so modest in size and power as to be barely noticeable into never-ending wars across the Greater Middle East and Africa, it would have seemed inconceivable.

Who would have believed a movie or novel in which that same power, without national enemies of any significance, would struggle unsuccessfully, year after year, to subdue scattered, lightly armed insurgents (aka "terrorists") across a crumbling region? Who could have imagined that every measure Washington took to assert its might only seemed to blow back (or blow somewhere, anyway)? Who would have believed that its full-scale invasion of one weak Middle Eastern country, its "mission accomplished" moment, would in the end prove a trip through "the gates of hell"? Who would have imagined that such an invasion could punch a hole in the oil heartlands of the region that, nearly sixteen years later, is still a bleeding wound, now seemingly beyond repair, or that it would set loose a principle of chaos and disintegration that seems to be spreading like a planetary Brexit?

Failed World?

As goes Britain, so, it seems, goes the world. Give Washington real credit for much of this. Those post–9/11 dreams of global domination shared by the top leadership of the Bush administration quickly proved wildly destructive and it's gotten no better since. Consider the vast swath of the planet where the devastation is most obvious: the Greater Middle East and North Africa. Then ask yourself: Are we still in the American Century? And if not, whose (or what) century are we in?

If you had told me in 1975, when the Vietnam War finally ended some thirty-four years after Luce wrote that essay and twenty-eight years before the United States invaded Iraq that, in 1979, Washington would involve itself in a decade-long war in Afghanistan, I would have been stunned. If you had told me in 1975 that, in 2001, it would invade that same country, launching a second Afghan War, with no end in sight, I wouldn't have believed you. A quarter century—and still counting—of American wars in a country that not so long before most Americans wouldn't have been able to locate on a map. If you had added that, starting in 1990, the United States would be involved in three successive wars in Iraq, the third of which would be ongoing almost a decade and a half after it began, I might have been speechless. And that's not to mention simultaneous interventions of various sorts in Somalia, Pakistan, Yemen, Libya, and Syria—none, by the way, by any normal standards successful.

If you were to do a little tabulation of the results of these years of American Century–ism across the Greater Middle East, you would discover a signature kind of chaos. In the early years of this century, officials of the Bush administration often referred to the region from China's western border to northern Africa as an "arc of instability." That phrase was their excuse for letting the US military loose there: to bring order and, of course, democracy to those lands. And with modest exceptions, it was indeed true that most of the Greater Middle East was then ruled by assorted repressive, autocratic, or regressive regimes. It was, however, still a reasonably orderly region. Now, it actually *is* an arc of instability, filled with states collapsing left and right, cities and towns that are being leveled, and terror outfits, each worse than the last, spreading in the regional rubble. Religious and ethnic divisions of every sort are sharpening and conflicts within countries, or what's left of them, are on the rise.

Most of the places where the United States has let its military power loose—Afghanistan, Iraq, Yemen, Libya, Somalia, and Syria—are now either failed or failing states. Under the circumstances, it might be reasonable to suggest that the very term "failed state" is outdated, and not just because it places all the blame for what's happened on the indigenous people of a country. After all, if the arc of instability is now in any way "united," it's mainly thanks to spreading terror groups and perhaps the Islamic State brand.

In the stunted view of Washington, the only policies imaginable in response to all this are highly militarized and call for more of the same: more air power in skies over distant battlefields, more boots on the ground, more private contractors and hired guns, more munitions (surprising amounts of which have since ended up in the hands not of allied forces, but of Washington's enemies), more special operations raids, more drone assassination campaigns, and at home, more surveillance, more powers for the national security state, more . . . well, you know the story.

For such a world, a new term is needed. Perhaps something like "failed region." This, it seems, is one thing that the American Century has come to mean seventy-five years after Henry Luce urged it into existence. And perhaps lurking as well is another phrase to describe another possibility, one not quite yet imaginable but the prospect of which is thoroughly chilling: failed world.

With this in mind, consider what Washington's so-called pivot to Asia could mean in the long run, or the US-NATO pivot to the Baltics and Eastern Europe. If huge swaths of the planet have begun to disintegrate in an era when the worst the United States faced in the way of opponents has been minority insurgencies and terror outfits, or more recently a terror caliphate, consider for a moment what kinds of chaos could come to regions where a potentially hostile great power remains.

And don't for a second think that, even if the Islamic State is finally defeated, worse can't emerge from the chaos and rubble of the failed region that it will leave behind. It can, and odds are it will.

All of this gives the very idea of an American Century new meaning. Can there be any question that this is not the century described by Henry Luce, nor the one that American political and military leaders dreamed of when the Soviet Union collapsed? What comes to mind instead is the sentiment Roman historian Tacitus attributed to Calgacus, a chieftain in what is now Scotland, speaking of the Roman conquests: "They make a desert and call it peace."

A recent UN report estimates that, in 2015, a record 65 million people were uprooted, mainly in the Greater Middle East. Tens of millions of them crossed borders and became refugees, including staggering numbers of children, many separated from their parents. So perhaps this really is the century of the lost child.

Has the American Age of Decline Begun?

He arrived with it on that Trump Tower escalator in the first moments of his campaign in June 2015 and it subsequently headlined his website, where it could be found emblazoned on an array of products from hats to t-shirts. You already know which line I mean: "Make America Great Again!" With that exclamation point ensuring that you won't miss the hyperbolic, Trumpian nature of its promise to return the country to its former glory days. The slogan encompassed the essence of Donald Trump's campaign for the presidency, of what he promised his followers and Americans generally—and yet, strangely enough, of all his lines, it's the one most taken for granted, the one that's been given the least thought and analysis. And that's a shame, because it represents something new in our American age. The problem, I suspect, is that what first catches the eye is the phrase "Make America Great" and then, of course, the exclamation point, while the single most important word in the slogan, historically speaking, is barely noted: "Again."

With that "again," Donald Trump crossed a line in American politics that represented a kind of psychological taboo for politicians of any stripe, from either party, including presidents and potential candidates for that position. He is the first American leader of recent times not to feel the need or obligation to insist that the United States, the "sole" superpower of Planet Earth, is an "exceptional" nation, an "indispensable" country, or even in an unqualified sense a "great" one. His claim has been the opposite: that, at present, America is anything but exceptional, indispensable, or great, and that he alone can make it "great again." In this claim lies a curiosity that, in a court of law, might be considered an admission of guilt. Yes, it says, this could be a different country, but—and here is the originality of the slogan—it is not great now. And in that admission-that-hasn't-been-seen-as-an-admission exists something new on the American landscape.

Donald Trump was the first person to run openly and without apology on a platform of American decline. "Make America Great Again!" is indeed an admission in the form of a boast. As he repeatedly told his audiences, America, the formerly great, is today a punching bag for China, Mexico. You don't have to agree with him on the specifics; what's interesting is the overall vision of a country lacking its former greatness.

"City upon a Hill"

Once upon a time, in a distant America, the words "greatest," "exceptional," and "indispensable" weren't even part of the political vocabulary. American presidents didn't bother to claim them, largely because America's wealth and global preeminence were indisputable. The 1950s and early 1960s were the post–World War II and pre-Vietnam "golden" years of US power. Despite a certain hysteria about the supposed dangers of domestic communists, few Americans then doubted the singularly unchallengeable greatness of the country. It was simply too self-evident for presidents to cite, hail, or praise.

Take, for instance, the speeches of John F. Kennedy. They are not littered with exceptionals, indispensables, or their equivalents. In a pre-inaugural speech he gave in January 1961 on the kind of government he planned to bring to Washington, for instance, he did cite the birth of a "great republic," the United States, and quoted Puritan John Winthrop on the desirability of creating a country that would be "a city upon a hill" to the rest of the world, with all of humanity's eyes upon it. In Kennedy's inaugural address ("Ask not what your country can do for you . . ."), he invoked a kind of unspoken greatness, saying, "We shall pay any price, bear any burden, meet any hardship, support any friend, oppose any foe to assure the survival and the success of liberty." It was then common to speak of the United States with pride as a "free nation" (as opposed to the "enslaved" ones of the Communist bloc) rather than an exceptional one. His only use of "great" was to invoke the US-led and Soviet Union–led blocs as "two great and powerful groups of nations."

Kennedy could even fall back on a certain modesty in describing the US role in the world (a modesty that, from Guatemala to Iran to Cuba, all too often did not carry over into actual policy in those years), saying in one speech, "We must face the fact that the United States is neither omnipotent or omniscient—that we are only 6 percent of the world's population—that we cannot impose our will upon the other

94 percent of mankind—that we cannot right every wrong or reverse each adversity—and that therefore there cannot be an American solution to every world problem." In that same speech, he typically spoke of America as "a great power"—but not "the greatest power."

None of this in any way implied a lack of national self-esteem. Rather, it implied a deep and abiding confidence in the overwhelming power and presence of this country, a confidence so unshakeable that there was no need to speak of it.

The Reagan Reboot

Defensiveness first crept into the American political lexicon with the unlikeliest of politicians: Ronald Reagan, the man who seemed like the least defensive, most genial guy on the planet. On this subject at least, he can be considered Trumpian before the advent of The Donald. After all, he was the man who (thanks to his ad writers) invented the political use of the word "again." It was first employed in 1984 in the seminal ad of Reagan's run for a second term in office. While that bucolic TV commercial was entitled "Prouder, Stronger, Better," its first line ever so memorably went, "It's morning again in America." ("Why would we ever want to return to where we were less than four short years ago?")

This was part of a post-Vietnam Reagan reboot, a time when the United States in Rambo-esque fashion was quite literally muscling up and over-arming itself in a major way. Reagan presided over "the biggest peacetime defense build-up in history" against what, referencing Star Wars, he called an "evil empire"—the Soviet Union. In those years, he also worked to rid the country of what was then termed "the Vietnam Syndrome" in part by rebranding that war a "noble cause." In a time when loss and decline were much on the American brain, he dismissed them both, even as he set America on a path toward the present moment of one-percent dysfunction, as a country that no longer invests fully in its own infrastructure, whose wages are stagnant, whose poor are a growth industry, whose wealth now flows eternally upward in a political environment awash in the money of the ultra-wealthy, and whose over-armed military continues to pursue a path of endless failure in the Greater Middle East.

Reagan, who spoke directly about American declinist thinking in his time—"Let's reject the nonsense that America is doomed to decline"—was hardly shy about his superlatives when it came to this country. He didn't hesitate to re-channel classic American rhetoric, ranging from Winthrop's "shining city upon a hill" (perhaps cribbed from Kennedy) in his farewell address, to Lincoln-esque ("the last best hope of man on Earth") invocations like "here in the heartland of America lives the hope of the world" or "in a world wracked by hatred, economic crisis, and political tension, America remains mankind's best hope."

And yet, in the 1980s, there were still limits to what needed to be said about America. The repeated superlatives of our own moment are, in fact, defensive markers on the declinist slope. The now-commonplace adjective "indispensable" as a stand-in for American greatness globally didn't arrive until Bill Clinton's secretary of state Madeleine Albright began using it in 1998. It only became an indispensable part of the rhetorical arsenal of American politicians a decade-plus into the twenty-first century, when the country's eerie dispensability became ever more apparent.

As for the United States being the planet's "exceptional" nation, for a phrase that now seems indelibly in the American grain, it's surprising how late it entered the presidential lexicon. As John Gans Jr. wrote in the *Atlantic* in 2011:

> [Obama] talked more about American exceptionalism than Presidents Reagan, George H. W. Bush, Bill Clinton, and George W. Bush combined: a search of UC Santa Barbara's exhaustive presidential records library finds that no president from 1981 to today uttered the phrase "American exceptionalism" except Obama. As *U.S. News'* Robert Schlesinger wrote, "American exceptionalism" is not a traditional part of presidential vocabulary. According to Schlesinger's search of public records, Obama is the only president in eighty-two years to use the term.

As the country has become politically shakier, the rhetoric about its greatness has only escalated in an American version of "the lady doth protest too much, methinks." Such descriptors have become the political equivalent of a litmus test: you couldn't be president or much of anything else without eternally testifying to your unwavering belief in American greatness.

As a result, the ultimate American narcissist, in promoting his own rise, has also openly promoted a version of decline and fall to striking numbers of Americans. For his followers, a major political figure has quit with the defensive BS and started saying it the way it is.

But don't furl the flag, shut down those offshore accounts, or start writing the complete history of American decline quite yet. After all, the United States still looms "lone" on an ever-more chaotic planet. Its wealth remains stunning, its economic clout something to behold, its tycoons the envy of the Earth, and its military beyond compare when it comes to how much and how destructively, even if not how successfully, they operate.

Still, make no mistake about it, Donald Trump is a harbinger, however bizarre, of a new American Century in which this country will indeed no longer be (with a bow to Muhammad Ali) "the greatest" or, for all but a shrinking crew, exceptional.

So, mark your calendars: 2016 is the official year the United States first went public as a declinist power—and for that you can thank Donald Trump.

America Last

In its own inside-out, upside-down way, it's almost wondrous to behold. As befits our president's wildest dreams, it may even prove to be a record for the ages, one for the history books. He was, after all, the candidate who sensed it first. When those he was running against, like the rest of Washington's politicians, were still insisting that the United States remained at the top of its game, not *an* but *the* "indispensable nation," the only truly "exceptional" one on the face of the Earth, he said nothing of the sort. He campaigned on America's decline, on this country's increasing lack of exceptionality, its potential dispensability. He ran on that single word "again" because (the implication was) it just isn't anymore. And he swore that he and he alone was the best shot

Americans, or at least non-immigrant white Americans, had at ever seeing those best of days again.

In that sense, he was our first declinist candidate for president and if that didn't reveal something during the election season, it should have. No question about it, he hit a chord, rang a bell, because out in the heartland it was possible to sense a deepening reality that wasn't evident in Washington. The wealthiest country on the planet, the most militarily powerful in the history of well, anybody, anywhere, anytime (or so we were repeatedly told), couldn't win a war, not even with the investment of trillions of taxpayer dollars, couldn't do anything but spread chaos by force of arms.

Meanwhile, at home, despite all that wealth, despite billionaires galore (including the one running for president), despite the transnational corporate heaven inhabited by Google and Facebook and Apple and the rest of the crew, parts of this country and its infrastructure were starting to feel distinctly (to use a word from another universe) Third Worldish. Trump sensed that, too. He regularly said things like: "We spent six trillion dollars in the Middle East, we got nothing. . . . And we have an obsolete plane system. We have obsolete airports. We have obsolete trains. We have bad roads. Airports." And this: "Our airports are like from a third-world country." And on the nation's crumbling infrastructure, he couldn't have been more on the mark.

In parts of the United States, white working-class and middle-class Americans could sense that the future was no longer theirs, that their children would not have a shot at what they had had, that they themselves increasingly didn't have a shot at what they had had. The American Dream seemed to be gaining an almost nightmarish sheen, given that the real value of the average wage of a worker hadn't increased since the 1970s, that the cost of a college education had gone through the roof and the educational debt burden for children with dreams of getting ahead was now staggering, that unions were cratering, and that income inequality was at a historic high. For them, the famed American Dream seemed ever more like someone else's trademarked property.

Indispensable? Exceptional? This country? Not anymore. Not as they were experiencing it. And because of that, Donald Trump won the lottery, entering the Oval Office with almost 50 percent of the vote and a fervent base of support for his promised program of doing it all over again, 1950s style.

It had been one hell of a pitch from the businessman billionaire. He had promised a future of stratospheric terrificness, of greatness on a historic scale. He promised to keep the evil ones—the rapists, job thieves, and terrorists—away, to wall them out, or toss them out, or ban them from ever traveling here. He also promised to set incredible records, as only a mega-businessman like him could conceivably do, the sort of all-American records this country hadn't seen in a long, long time.

And though it's still early in the Trump era, it seems as if, on one score at least, he could deliver something for the record books going back to the times when those recording the acts of rulers were scratching them out in clay or wax. At this point, there's at least a chance that Donald Trump might preside over the most precipitous decline of a truly dominant power in history, one only recently considered at the height of its glory. It could prove to be a fall for the ages. Admittedly, that other superpower of the Cold War era, the Soviet Union, imploded in 1991 in about the fastest way imaginable to leave the global stage. Still, despite the "evil empire" talk of that era, the USSR was always the secondary, the weaker of the two superpowers. At its height, it was never Rome, or Spain, or Great Britain.

When it comes to the United States, we're talking about a country that not so long ago saw itself as the only great power left. It was the one still standing, triumphant, in the wake of great-power rivalries that went back to a time when the wooden warships of various European states first broke out into a larger world and began to conquer it. It stood by itself, as its proponents liked to claim at the time, at the end of history.

TWO

Empire of Chaos

Looking back on almost fifteen years in which the United States has been engaged in something like permanent war in the Greater Middle East and parts of Africa, one thing couldn't be clearer: the planet's sole superpower, with a military funded and armed like none other and a "defense" budget larger than the next seven countries combined (three times as large as the number two spender, China), has managed to accomplish absolutely nothing. Unless you consider an expanding series of failed states, spreading terror movements, wrecked cities, countries hemorrhaging refugees, and the like as accomplishments.

In these years, no goal of Washington—not a single one—has been accomplished by war. This has proven true even when, in the first flush of death and destruction, victory, or at least success, was hailed, as it was in Afghanistan in 2001 ("You helped Afghanistan liberate itself—for a second time," Secretary of Defense Donald Rumsfeld told US special operations forces), Iraq in 2003 ("Mission Accomplished"), or Libya in 2011 ("We came, we saw, he died," as Hillary Clinton said of the death of autocrat Muammar Gaddafi).

Of all forms of American military might in this period, none may have been more destructive or less effective than air power. US drones, for instance, have killed incessantly in these years, racking up thousands of dead Pakistanis, Afghans, Iraqis, Yemenis, Syrians, and others, including top terror leaders and their lieutenants as well as significant numbers of civilians and even children, and yet the movements they were sent to destroy from the top down have only proliferated. From Afghanistan in 2001 to Syria and Iraq today, the US Air Force has been repeatedly loosed in a region in which those on the ground are helpless against air power, without challenge and with utter freedom of the skies. Yet, other than dead civilians and militants and a great deal of rubble, the long-term results have been remarkably pitiful.

From all of this no conclusions ever seem to be drawn, and after almost fifteen years of it, we know just where such "successes" lead: to even grimmer, more brutal, more effective terror movements. And yet, the military approach remains the American approach *du jour* in the twenty-first century.

For the country that has, like no other on the planet in these years, unleashed its military again and again thousands of miles from its "homeland," in actions ranging from large-scale invasions and occupations to small-scale raids and drone assassination strikes, absolutely nothing has come up roses. From China's Central Asian border to North Africa, the region that Washington officials began referring to as an "arc of instability" soon after 9/11 and that they hoped to garrison and dominate forever has only become more unstable, less amenable to American power, and ever more chaotic.

By its very nature, war produces chaos, but in other eras, particularly for great powers, war has also meant influence or dominance, creating the basis for reshaping or controlling whole regions. None of this seems in the cards today. It would be reasonable to conclude, however provisionally, from America's grand military experiment of this century that, no matter the military strength at your command, war no longer translates into power. For Washington, war has somehow been decoupled from its once expected results, no matter what weaponry has been brought to bear or what kind of generalship was exercised.

An Arms Race of One

Given that, sooner or later, the results of any experiment should be taken into account and actions recalibrated accordingly, here's what's curious. Just recall the fervent pledges of the presidential candidates in the 2016 Republican debates to "rebuild" the military, and you'll sense the immense pressure in Washington not to recalibrate anything. If you want the definition of a Trumpian bad deal, consider that all of these other players were eager to pour further staggering sums into preparations for future military endeavors not so different from the present ones. And don't just blame the Republicans. Such behavior is now hardwired into Washington's entire political class.

The essential failure of air power in these years of military action has yielded the F-35 Joint Strike Fighter, a plane once expected to cost in the $200 billion range, but whose price tag is now estimated at a trillion dollars or more over the course of its lifetime. It will, that is, be the most expensive weapons system in history. Air power's powerlessness to achieve Washington's ends has also yielded the newly unveiled Long-Range Strike Bomber, for which the Pentagon has already made a down payment of $55 billion to Northrop Grumman (add in the usual future cost overruns and that sum is expected to crest the $100 billion mark long before the plane is actually built). Or at the level of planetary destruction, consider the three-decade, trillion-dollar upgrading of the nuclear arsenal now underway and scheduled to include, among other things, smaller, more accurate "smart" nukes—that is, first-use weaponry that might indeed be brought to future battlefields.

That none of this fits our world of war today should be—but isn't—obvious, at least not in Washington. Not only has military action of just about any sort been decoupled from success of just about any sort, but the unbelievably profitable industry of weapons production has been woven into the fabric of the capital and the political process. The worse we do militarily, that is, the more frenetically and expensively we build.

For the conspiratorial-minded, it's easy enough to see the growing chaos and collapse in the Greater Middle East as purposeful, as what the military-industrial complex desires; nothing, in other words, succeeds for weapons makers like failure. The more failed states, the more widespread the terror groups, the greater the need to arm ourselves and, as the planet's leading arms dealer, others. This is, however, the thinking of outsiders. For the weapons makers and the rest of that complex, failure or success may increasingly be beside the point. If the United States were to become triumphant in an orderly future Greater Middle East, the same Republican candidates would still be calling for a build-up of the military to maintain our victorious stance globally.

For proof of this, you only need to recall the moment the Soviet Union collapsed. That should have been the finale of a long history of arms races among competing great powers. What seemed like the last arms race of all between the two superpowers of the Cold War, the one that brought the planet to the brink of annihilation, had just ended. When the Soviet Union disappeared and Washington dissolved in a riot of shock and triumphalism, only one imperial force—"the sole superpower"—remained. And yet, despite a brief flurry of talk about Americans harvesting a "peace dividend" in a world bereft of major enemies, what continued to be harvested were new weapons systems. An arms race of one rolled right along.

And it goes right on today in an almost unimaginably different world. Now, a quarter of a century later, militarily speaking, two other nations could be considered great powers. One of them, China, is indeed building up its military and acting in more provocative ways in nearby seas. However, not since its disastrous 1979 border war with Vietnam has it used its military outside its own borders in a conflict of any kind.

The Russians are another matter, and they alone seem to be making an imperial success of warfare—translating, that is, war-making into power, prestige, and dominance. The Russians in Syria have essentially followed the path Washington pioneered in this century, loosing air power, advisers, and proxy forces on an embattled country. Their bombing campaign and that of the allied Syrian Air Force have been doing in spades what air power generally does: blow away stuff on the ground, including hospitals, schools, and the like. While things look relatively sunny for the Russians in Syria (as long as your view is an airborne one), give it a year or two or three. But what exactly will such "success" translate into, even if a Bashar al-Assad regime regains significant power in a country that, in most senses, has simply ceased to exist? Its cities, after all, are in varying states of destruction, a startling 11.5 percent of its people are estimated to have been killed or injured, and a significant portion of the rest transformed into exiles and refugees (with more being produced all the time).

Even if the Islamic State and other rebel and insurgent groups, ranging from those backed by the United States to those linked to al-Qaeda, can be "defeated," what is Russia likely to inherit in the Middle East? What, in far better circumstances, did the United States inherit in Afghanistan or Iraq? What horrendous new movements will be born from such a "victory"? It's a nightmare just to think about.

Unlike the United States, Vladimir Putin's Russia is no superpower. Despite its superpower-style nuclear arsenal and its great-power-ish military, it's a rickety energy state shaken by bargain-basement oil prices. Economically, it doesn't have the luxury of waste that the United States has when it comes to military experimentation.

Generally speaking, in these last years, war has meant destruction and nothing but destruction. It's true that from the point of view of movements like al-Qaeda and the Islamic State, the chaos of great-power-war is a godsend. Even if such groups never win a victory in the traditional sense (as the Islamic State has), they can't lose, no matter how many of their leaders and followers are wiped out. In the same way, no matter how many immediate successes Washington has in pursuit of its war on terror, it can't win (and in the end neither, it seems, can Russia).

Has War Outlived Its Usefulness?

Relatively early in the post–9/11 presidency of George W. Bush, it became apparent that his top officials had confused military power with power itself. They had come to venerate force and its possible uses in a way that only men who had never been to war possibly could. (Secretary of State Colin Powell was the sole exception to this rule of thumb.) In the US military, they were fundamentalists and true believers, convinced that unleashing its uniquely destructive capabilities would open the royal road to control of the Greater Middle East and possibly the planet as well.

. In this—and in themselves—they were supremely confident. As an unnamed "senior adviser" to the president (later identified as Bush-confidant Karl Rove) told journalist Ron Suskind, "We're an empire now, and when we act, we create our own reality. And while you're studying that reality—judiciously, as you will—we'll act again, creating other new realities, which you can study too, and that's how things will sort out. We're history's actors . . . and you, all of you, will be left to just study what we do."

Ever since then, no small thanks to the military-industrial complex, military power has remained the option of choice, even when it became clear that it could not produce a minimal version of what the Bush crew hoped for. In a period when military power of the first order doesn't seem to translate into a thing of value, American economic (and cultural) power still does. The realm of the dollar, not the F-35, still rules the planet.

Could it be that war has in the most literal sense outlived its usefulness, at least for the United States? Could it be that the nature of war—possibly any war, but certainly the highly mechanized, high-tech, top-dollar form that the United States fights—is now all unintended consequences?

The Taliban is at present in control of more territory than at any time since the US invasion and is gaining an ever-firmer grip on contested Helmand Province in the heart of the country's poppy-growing region (and the staggering drug funds that go with it). In that same province, only about half of the "on duty" Afghan security forces the United States trained, equipped, and largely funded (to the tune of more than $65 billion over the years) were reportedly even present.

On his way into retirement, the American commander there, General John Campbell, vigorously urged the Obama administration to expand its operations in that country. ("I'm not going to leave," he said, "without making sure my leadership understands that there are things we need to do.") In this, he's been in good company. Behind the scenes, "top US military commanders" have reportedly been talking up a renewed, decades-long commitment to Afghanistan and its security forces. As Campbell headed off stage, General John Nicholson Jr., beginning his fourth tour of duty in Afghanistan, officially took command of the International Security Assistance Force. Though it wasn't a major news item, he happens to be its seventeenth commander in the many years of Washington's Afghan War. If this pattern holds, by 2030 that international force, dominated by the United States, will have had thirty-four commanders and have fought, by at least a multiple of two, the longest war in our history.

How Much, How Many, How Often, and How Destructively

In Iraq and Syria, it's been mission creep all the way. The B-52s had barely made it to the battle zone for the first time in 2016 before they were in the air, attacking Islamic State militants. American firebases are being built ever closer to the front lines. The number of special ops forces continues to edge up. American weapons flow in (ending up in god knows whose hands). American trainers and advisers follow in ever increasing numbers, and those numbers are repeatedly fiddled with to deemphasize how many of them are actually there. Private contractors are beginning to arrive in numbers never to be counted. The local forces being trained or retrained have their usual problems in battle. American troops and advisers who were never, never going to be "in combat" or have "boots on the ground" themselves now have their boots distinctly on the ground in combat situations. The first American casualties are dribbling in. Meanwhile, conditions in tottering Iraq and the former nation of Syria by the week grow ever murkier, more chaotic, and less amenable to any solution American officials might care for.

And Washington's response to all this? It's perfectly clear what their sole imaginable response can be: sending in yet more weapons, boots, air power, special ops types, trainers, advisers, private contractors, drones, and funds to conflict zones across significant swaths of the planet. Above all, there can be no serious thought, discussion, or debate about how such a militarized approach to our world might have contributed to the very problems it is meant to solve. Not in our nation's capital, anyway.

The only questions to be debated are how much, how many, how often, and how destructively. The only "antiwar" positions possible in Washington, where accusations of weakness or wimpishness are a dime a dozen and considered lethal to a political career, are how much less of more we can afford, militarily speaking, or how much more of somewhat less we can settle for when it comes to militarized death and destruction. Never is a genuine version of less or a none-at-all option really on that table where, it's said, all policy options are kept.

Washington's attachment—financial, tactical, and strategic—to the US military, and its supposed solutions to more or less all problems in what used to be called "foreign policy," should by now be categorized as addictive. Otherwise, how can you explain the last decade and a half in which no military action, from Afghanistan to Iraq, Yemen to Libya, worked out even half-well in the long run (or, often enough, in the short run), and yet the US military remains the option of first, not last, resort in just about every situation?

Remember that the president who came into office swearing he would end a disastrous war and occupation in Iraq oversaw a new war in an even broader region that included Iraq, a country that is no longer quite a country, and Syria. Meanwhile, in the other war he inherited, Barack Obama almost immediately launched a military-backed "surge" of American forces, the only real argument being over whether forty thousand (or even as many as eighty thousand) new US troops would be sent into Afghanistan or, as the "antiwar" president finally decided, a mere thirty thousand (which made him an absolute wimp to his opponents). That was in 2009. Part of that surge involved an announcement that the withdrawal of American combat forces would begin in 2011. Yet that withdrawal has once again been halted in favor of what the military has taken to privately calling a "generational approach"—that is, US forces remaining in Afghanistan at least well into the 2020s.

Hawkish Washington

There is simply no compelling evidence that the usual military solutions have worked or are likely to work in any imaginable sense in the present conflicts across the Greater Middle East and Africa. In fact, they have clearly played a major role in the creation of the present disaster, and yet there is no place at all in our political system for genuinely antiwar figures (as there was in the Vietnam era, when a massive antiwar movement created space for such politics). Antiwar opinions and activities have now been driven to the peripheries of the political system along with a word like, say, "peace," which you will be hard-pressed to find, even rhetorically, in the language of "wartime" Washington.

If a history were to be written of how the military became Washington's drug of choice, it would undoubtedly have to begin in the Cold War era. It was, however, in the prolonged moment of triumphalism that followed the Soviet Union's collapse in 1991 that it gained its present position of unquestioned dominance.

In those days, people were still speculating about whether the country would reap a "peace dividend" from the end of the Cold War. If there was ever a moment when the diversion of money from the military and the national security state to domestic concerns might have seemed like a no-brainer, that was it. After all, except for a couple of rickety "rogue states" like North Korea and Saddam Hussein's Iraq, where exactly were this country's enemies to be found? And why should such a muscle-bound military continue to gobble up tax dollars at such a staggering rate in a reasonably peaceable world?

In the decade or so that followed, however, Washington's dreams turned out to run in a very different direction—toward a "war dividend" instead. The crew who entered the White House with George W. Bush in a deeply contested election in 2000 had already been mainlining the military drug for years. To them, this seemed a planet ripe for the taking. When 9/11 hit, it loosed their dreams of conquest and control, and their faith in a military that they believed to be unstoppable. Given the previous century of successful anti-imperial and national independence movements, anyone should have known that, no matter the armaments at hand, resistance was an inescapable reality on Planet Earth.

Thanks to such predictable resistance, the imperial dreamscape of the Busheviks would prove a fantasy of the first order, even if, in that post–9/11 moment, it passed for bedrock (neo)realism. The United States was to "take the gloves off" and release a military machine so beyond compare that nothing would be capable of standing in its path. So the dream went, so the drug spoke. Don't forget that the greatest military blunder (and crime) of this century, the invasion of Iraq, wasn't supposed to be the end of something, but merely its beginning. With Iraq in hand and garrisoned, Washington was to take down Iran and sweep up what Russian property from the Cold War era still remained in the Middle East. (Think: Syria.)

A decade and a half later, those dreams have been shattered, and yet the drug still courses through the bloodstream, the military bands play on, and the march to . . . well, who knows where . . . continues. In a way, we do know where, and we've already been shown a spectacle of what "victory" might look like once the Greater Middle East is finally "liberated" from the Islamic State.

The descriptions of one widely hailed victory over that brutal crew in Iraq—the liberation of the city of Ramadi by a US-trained elite Iraqi counterterrorism force backed by artillery and American air power—are devastating. Aided and abetted by Islamic State militants igniting or demolishing whole neighborhoods of that city, the look of Ramadi retaken should give us a grim sense of where the region is heading.

Here's how the Associated Press described the scene, four months after the city fell:

> This is what victory looks like . . . in the once thriving Haji Ziad Square, not a single structure still stands. Turning in every direction yields a picture of devastation. A building that housed a pool hall and ice cream shops—reduced to rubble. A row of money changers and motorcycle repair garages—obliterated, a giant bomb crater in its place. The square's Haji Ziad Restaurant, beloved for years by Ramadi residents for its grilled meats—flattened. The restaurant was so popular its owner built a larger, fancier

branch across the street three years ago. That, too, is now a pile of concrete and twisted iron rods.

The destruction extends to nearly every part of Ramadi, once home to 1 million people and now virtually empty.

With oil prices still deeply depressed, Iraq essentially has no money to rebuild Ramadi or anyplace else. And as such "victories" multiply, versions of similar devastation are spreading across the region.

One likely end result of the thoroughly militarized process that began with the invasion of Iraq (if not of Afghanistan) is already visible: a region shattered and in ruins, filled with uprooted and impoverished people. In such circumstances, it may not even matter if the Islamic State is defeated. Just imagine what Mosul, Iraq's second-largest city and still in the Islamic State's hands, will be like if the long-promised offensive to liberate it is ever truly launched. Now, try to imagine that movement itself destroyed, with its "capital," Raqqa, turned into another set of ruins. What exactly is likely to emerge from such a future nightmare?

Their Precision Weaponry and Ours

On the morning of September 11, 2001, al-Qaeda launched its four-plane air force against the United States. On board were its precision weapons: nineteen suicidal hijackers. One of those planes, thanks to the resistance of its passengers, crashed in a Pennsylvania field. The other three hit their targets—the two towers of the World Trade Center in New York City and the Pentagon in Washington, DC—with the kind of "precision" we now associate with the laser-guided weaponry of the US Air Force.

From its opening salvo this conflict has been an air war. With its 75 percent success rate, al-Qaeda's 9/11 mission was a historic triumph, accurately striking three out of what assumedly were its four chosen targets. (Though no one knows just where that plane in Pennsylvania was heading, undoubtedly it was either the Capitol or the White House to complete the taking out of the icons of American financial, military, and political power.) In the process, almost three thousand people who had no idea they were in the bombsights of an obscure movement on the other side of the planet were slaughtered.

It was a barbaric, if daring, plan and an atrocity of the first order. Today, such suicidal acts with similar "precision" weaponry (though without the air power component) continue to be unleashed across the Greater Middle East, Africa, and sometimes elsewhere, taking a terrible toll—from a soccer game in Iraq to a Kurdish wedding party in southeastern Turkey (where the "weapon" may have been a boy).

The effect of the September 11 attacks was stunning. Though the phrase would have no resonance or meaning (outside of military circles) until the invasion of Iraq began a year and a half later, 9/11 qualifies as perhaps the most successful example of "shock-and-awe" tactics imaginable. The attack was promptly encapsulated in screaming headlines as the "Pearl Harbor of the Twenty-First Century" or a "New Day of Infamy," and the images of those towers crumbling in New York at what was almost instantly called "Ground Zero" (as if the city had experienced a nuclear strike) were replayed again and again to a stunned world.

In Washington, the vice president headed for a deep underground bunker; the secretary of defense, speaking to his aides at the damaged Pentagon, urged them to "Go massive. Sweep it all up. Things related and not" (the first hint of the coming decision to invade Iraq and take out Saddam Hussein); and the president, who was reading a children's story, *The Pet Goat*, to a class of elementary school students in Sarasota, Florida, while the attacks took place, boarded Air Force One and promptly headed away from Washington. Just three days later, though, he would appear at Ground Zero, bullhorn in hand, where he would swear that "the people who knocked these buildings down will hear all of us soon!"

Within days, he had announced a "war on terror." And on October 7, 2001, less than a month after the attacks, the Bush administration would launch its own air war, dispatching B-2 stealth bombers with satellite-guided precision weaponry from the United States as well as B-1 and B-52 long-range bombers from the British Indian Ocean island of Diego Garcia, supplemented by strike aircraft from two aircraft carriers and about fifty Tomahawk cruise missiles fired from ships. And this was just its initial air riposte to al-Qaeda (though the most significant parts of the attack were, in fact, aimed at taking out the Taliban regime that then controlled much of Afghanistan). By the end of December 2001, 17,500 bombs and other munitions had rained down on Afghanistan, 57 percent of which were reportedly "precision-guided" smart weapons. Released as well, however, were perfectly dumb bombs and cluster munitions filled with "soda-can-like" bomblets which scatter over a wide area, don't all explode on contact, and so remain around for civilians to mistakenly pick up.

That air war has never ended. In Afghanistan, for instance, in just the first four years of the Obama administration (2009–2012), more than 18,000 munitions were released over the country. And in 2017, B-52s, those old Vietnam workhorses, took to the air again as air sorties there ramped up against surging Taliban and Islamic State militants.

And that's just to begin to describe the never-ending nature of the American air war that has spread across the Greater Middle East and parts of Africa in these years. In response to al-Qaeda's brief set of air strikes in 2001, Washington launched an air campaign that has yet to end, involving the use of hundreds of thousands of bombs and missiles, many of a "precision" sort but some as dumb as they come, against a growing array of enemies. Today, American bombs and missiles are landing on targets in not one but seven largely Muslim countries (Afghanistan, Iraq, Libya, Pakistan, Somalia, Syria, and Yemen).

What are we to make of al-Qaeda's and Washington's "precision" air campaigns? Here are some thoughts.

SUCCESS AND FAILURE

Without a hint of exaggeration, you could say that, at the cost of $400,000 to $500,000, al-Qaeda's 9/11 air assault created Washington's multi-trillion-dollar Global War on Terror. With a microscopic, hijacked air force and a single morning's air campaign, that group provoked an administration already dreaming of global domination into launching a worldwide air war (with a significant ground component) that would turn the Greater Middle East—then a relatively calm, if largely autocratic, region—into a morass of conflicts. This was the brilliance of Osama bin Laden. Seldom has so little air power (or perhaps power of any sort) been leveraged quite so purposefully into such sweeping results. It may represent the most successful use of strategic bombing—that is, air power aimed at the civilian population of, and morale in, an enemy country—in history.

In contrast, with only a slight hint of exaggeration, you might also conclude that seldom has an air campaign without end proven quite so unsuccessful. On September 11, 2001, al-Qaeda was the most modest of forces with militant followers in perhaps the low thousands in Afghanistan and tiny numbers of scattered supporters elsewhere on the planet. Now, there are al-Qaeda spin-offs and wannabe outfits, often thriving, from Pakistan to Yemen, Syria to North Africa, and of course the "brand" of the Islamic State, that self-proclaimed "caliphate" of Abu Bakr al-Baghdadi, has spread to groups from Afghanistan to Libya.

The American air campaign, which has certainly killed enough terror leaders, "lieutenants," "militants," and others over these years, has shown no ability to halt the process and arguably has ploughed remarkably fertile ground for it. Yet the bombs continue to fall. It's a curious record in the generally disappointing annals of air power and well worth considering in more detail.

BOMBS AWAY!

By the end of 2015, the rate of US bomb and missile use over Iraq and Syria was so high that stockpiles of both were reportedly depleted. Air Force Chief of Staff General Mark Welsh said, "We're expending munitions faster than we can replenish them. B-1s have dropped bombs in record numbers. . . . We need the funding in place to ensure we're prepared for the long fight. This is a critical need."

And this situation carried into 2016, as bombing runs over Syria and Iraq only seemed to rise. Even though both Boeing, which makes the Joint Direct Attack Munition, and Lockheed Martin, which produces the Hellfire missile (so crucial to Washington's drone assassination campaigns), significantly stepped up production of those weapons, there were still shortfalls.

Fears have risen that at some point there might not be enough munitions for the wars being fought, in part because of the expense involved in producing various kinds of precision weaponry.

The numbers associated with the US air campaign that is the heart and soul of Operation Inherent Resolve, the war against the Islamic State in Iraq and Syria begun in August 2014, are striking. As 2015 ended, scholar Micah Zenko estimated (based on figures released by Air Force Central Command) that 23,144 bombs and missiles had been dropped on both countries by the Air Force that year (and another 5,500 by coalition partners) in what he calls Washington's "kill 'em all with airstrikes" strategy—which, he adds, "is not working." In fact, studies of the "kingpin strategy" or "decapitation" as it's sometimes known—attempts to destroy terror groups from the top down—indicate that it has had anything but the desired effect.

BARBARISM AND CIVILIZATION
(OR, THEIR PRECISION AND OURS)

Al-Qaeda was quite precise in its assault on the American homeland. Its goal was clearly to take out both iconic structures and whoever might be in them. In the process, it intended to horrify and provoke. On both counts, it was successful beyond what even its planners could have imagined. With perfect accuracy, the world branded this as barbarism of the first order.

Al-Qaeda's "precision" tactics and those of its successor organizations, from al-Qaeda in the Arabian Peninsula to the Islamic State, have not changed greatly over the years. Their precision weapons are sent into the heartlands of civilian life, as in that August 2016 wedding ceremony in Turkey where a suicide bomber, possibly a boy outfitted with explosives, killed fifty-four, including twenty-two children under fourteen, to create anger and outrage. The barbarity of this form of warfare is aimed, as ISIS says, at destroying the "gray zone" of our world, and creating instead an ever-more us-vs.-them planet. At the same time, such attacks are meant to provoke the powers-that-be into striking back in ways that will create sympathy for ISIS in its world, as well as spark the kinds of conflict and chaos in which such organizations are likely, in the long run, to thrive. Osama bin Laden understood this early on; others have grasped his point since.

But what about our version of—to use a word seldom applied to us—barbarity? Take the Bush administration's official "shock and awe" air campaign that began the invasion of Iraq on March 19–20, 2003. It involved an overwhelming display of air power, including fifty "decapitation" strikes meant to take out top Iraqi leaders. In fact, not a single leader was touched. According to Human Rights Watch, those strikes instead killed "dozens of civilians." In less than two weeks, at least eight thousand precision-guided bombs and missiles were loosed on Iraq. Some, of course, missed their precise targets but killed civilians; others hit their targets in crowded urban areas or even villages and had the same result. A small number of Tomahawk missiles of the more than seven hundred fired in those first weeks of war, at a cost of $750,000 apiece, missed Iraq altogether and landed in Iran, Saudi Arabia, and Turkey.

In that brief period when Baghdad was taken and the invasion declared a success, 863 US planes were committed to the operation, more than 24,000 air "sorties" were conducted and, by one estimate, more than 2,700 civilians died under them—that is, nearly a Twin Towers–full of Iraqi non-combatants. In the first six years of the air war in Iraq, one study published in the *New England Journal of Medicine* found that "46 percent of the victims of US air strikes whose gender could be determined were female and 39 percent were children."

Similarly, in December 2003, Human Rights Watch reported that in Iraq American and British planes had dropped or artillery had fired "almost 13,000 cluster munitions, containing nearly two million submunitions, that killed or wounded more than 1,000 civilians." And the likelihood was that more died from scattered, unexploded bomblets in the months or years thereafter, including curious children. In fact, the United States dropped cluster bombs in Afghanistan as well (with undoubtedly similar results), and in recent times has sold them to the Saudis for their profligate air campaign in Yemen.

To grasp the scale of that 2003 air assault, consider the USS *Abraham Lincoln*, the aircraft carrier positioned off the coast of San Diego so that President George W. Bush could make a flamboyant landing on it that May 1 and, under a banner reading "Mission Accomplished," declare that "major combat operations in Iraq have ended," and that the United States and its allies had "prevailed." As it happened, the carrier had just returned from a ten-month deployment in the Persian Gulf during which its planes had flown some 16,500 missions and dropped approximately 1.6 million pounds of bombs. And that was just one part of the overall air campaign against Saddam Hussein's forces.

It is now obvious that the Bush administration's shock-and-awe strikes and the invasion that followed were neither precise nor effective in the short or the long run. So shouldn't it be self-evident that an air war, which has helped turn embattled Iraqi cities into rubble, and shows no sign of ending any time soon, is barbaric?

Put in more graphic fashion: Does anyone doubt that the Kurdish wedding slaughter (assumedly by an Islamic State suicide bomber) was a barbaric act? If not, then what are we to make of the eight documented cases—largely ignored in the United States—in which US air power eviscerated similar wedding parties in three countries (Afghanistan, Iraq, and Yemen) between December 2001 and December 2013, killing in total almost 300 celebrants?

But in our world, there is only one type of barbarism: theirs.

The Wars Come Home

Since the moment of the invasion of Afghanistan in October 2001, everything the American military has touched has turned to dust. Nations across the Greater Middle East and Africa collapsed under the weight of American interventions or those of its allies, and terror movements, one grimmer than the next, spread remarkably unchecked. Afghanistan is now a disaster zone; Yemen, wracked by civil war, a brutal US-backed Saudi air campaign, and various ascendant terror groups, is essentially no more; Iraq, at best, is a riven sectarian nation; Syria barely exists; Libya, too, is hardly a state these days; and Somalia is a set of fiefdoms and terror movements. All in all, it's quite a record for the mightiest power on the planet, which has been unable to impose its military will or order of any sort on any state or even any group, wherever it has chosen to act in these years. It's hard to think of a historical precedent for this.

Meanwhile, from the shattered lands of the empire of chaos stream refugees by the millions in numbers not seen since vast swaths of the globe were left in rubble at the end of World War II. Startling percentages of the populations of various failed and failing states, including stunning numbers of children, have been driven into internal exile or been sent fleeing across borders and, from Afghanistan to North Africa to Europe, they are shaking up the planet in unsettling ways (as they, in their spectral form, shook up the 2016 election here in the United States).

It's something of a cliché to say that, sooner or later, the frontier wars of any empire come home to haunt the imperial heartland in curious ways. Certainly, such has been the case for our wars on the peripheries. In various ways—from the militarization of the police to the loosing of spy drones in American skies and of surveillance technology previously tested on distant battlefields—America's post–9/11 conflicts have returned to "the homeland," even if, most of the time, we have paid remarkably little attention to this phenomenon.

What Election 2016 made clear was that the empire of chaos has not just remained a characteristic of the planet's backlands. It's with us in the United States, right here, right now. And it's come home in a fashion that no one has yet truly tried to grapple with. Can't you feel the deep and spreading sense of disorder that lay at the heart of the bizarre presidential campaign that roiled this country, brought the most extreme kinds of racism and xenophobia back into the mainstream, and with Donald Trump's election, may never really end? Using the term of tradecraft that Chalmers Johnson borrowed from the CIA and popularized, think of this as, in some strange fashion, the ultimate in "imperial blowback."

There's a history to be written of how such disorder came home, of how it warped the American system and our democratic form of governance, of how a process that began decades ago not in the stew of defeat or disaster but in a moment of unparalleled imperial triumph undermined so much.

The empire of chaos began with a victory so stunning, so complete, and so imperial that it essentially helped drive the other superpower, that "evil empire" the Soviet Union, to self-destruct. It began, in fact, with the desire of Jimmy Carter's national security advisor, Zbigniew Brzezinski, to give the Soviets a bloody nose, or to be more precise, a taste of America's Vietnam experience: to trap the Red Army in an Afghan quagmire.

In 1979, the CIA started a massive, decade-long covert program to fund, arm, and train fundamentalist opponents of the left-wing Afghan government in Kabul and of the occupying Red Army. To do so, it fatefully buddied up with two unsavory "allies": with the Saudis, who were ready to sink their oil money into support for Afghan mujahedeen fighters of the most extreme sort, and with the Pakistani intelligence service, the ISI, which was intent on controlling events in that land, no matter the nature of the cast of characters it found available.

In the fashion of Vietnam for the Americans, Afghanistan would prove to be what Soviet leader Mikhail Gorbachev called "the bleeding wound" for the Russians. A decade later, the Red Army would limp home in defeat and within two years a hollowed-out Soviet Union, never as strong as Washington imagined, would collapse, in a triumph so stunning that the American political elite initially couldn't take it in. After almost half a century, the Cold War was over; one of the two remaining "superpowers" had left the global stage in defeat; and for the first time since Europeans set out on wooden ships to conquer distant parts of the globe, only a single great power was left standing on the planet.

Given the history of those centuries past, the dreams of Bush-Cheney & Co. about how the United States would dominate the world as no power before, not even the Romans or the British, had ever done seemed to make a certain sense. But in that triumph of 1989 lay the seeds as well of future chaos. To take down the Soviets, the CIA, in tandem with the Saudis and the Pakistanis, had armed and built up groups of extreme Islamists, who, it turned out, had no intention of going away once the Soviets were driven from Afghanistan. In those decisions lay the genesis of the 9/11 attacks and, in some curious fashion, even perhaps the rise of a presidential candidate, and now president, so bizarre that, despite the billions of words expended on him, he remains a phenomenon beyond understanding.

Imperial Overreach and the Rise of the National Security State

Those seeds, first planted in Afghan and Pakistani soil in 1979, led to the attacks of September 11, 2001. That day was the very definition of chaos brought to the imperial heartland, and it spurred the emergence of a new, post-constitutional governing structure through the expansion of the national security state to monumental proportions, and a staggering version of imperial overreach. On the basis of the supposed need to keep Americans safe from terrorism (and essentially nothing else), that national security state would balloon into a dominant—and dominantly funded—set of institutions at the heart of American political life. In these years, that state-within-a-state became the unofficial fourth branch of government, at a moment when two of the others—Congress and the courts, or at least the Supreme Court—were faltering.

The attacks of 9/11 also gave free rein to the Bush administration's stunningly ambitious, ultimately disastrous Global War on Terror, and over-the-top fantasies about establishing a military-enforced *Pax Americana*, first in the Middle East and then perhaps worldwide. With it were unleashed the subsequent wars in Afghanistan and Iraq, a drone assassination program across significant parts of the planet, the building of an unprecedented global surveillance state, the spread of a kind of secrecy so all-encompassing that much of government activity became unknowable to "the people," and a kind of imperial overreach that sent literally trillions of dollars (often via warrior corporations) tumbling into the abyss. All of these were chaos-creating factors.

At the same time, the basic needs of many Americans went increasingly unattended, of those at least who weren't part of a Gilded Age one-percent sucking up American wealth in an extraordinary fashion. The one-percenters then repurposed some of those trickle-up funds for the buying and selling of politicians, again taking place in an atmosphere of remarkable secrecy. In turn, that stream of Supreme Court–approved funds changed the nature of, and perhaps the very idea of, what an election was.

Meanwhile, parts of the heartland were being hollowed out, while— even as the military continued to produce trillion-dollar boondoggle weapons systems—the country's inadequately funded infrastructure began to crumble in a way that once would have been inconceivable. Similarly, the non-security-state part of the government—Congress in particular—began to falter and wither. One of the country's two great political parties launched a scorched-earth campaign against governing representatives of the other's, and against the very idea of governing in a reasonably democratic fashion or getting much of anything done at all. That party subsequently shattered into disorderly, competing factions that grew ever more extreme and produced what is a unique celebrity presidency of chaos.

Abroad, Trump's unexpected success will only encourage the rise of right-wing nationalist movements and the further political fragmentation of this planet of increasing disorder. Meanwhile, the American military (promised a vast further infusion of funds by The Donald during his campaign) will continue to try to impose its version of order in distant lands. All of this should shock no one. Here, however, is a potentially shocking question that has to be asked: With Donald Trump's election, has the American "experiment" run its course?

THREE

The Election from Hell

In its halcyon days, Washington could overthrow governments, install shahs and other rulers, do more or less what it wanted across significant parts of the globe and reap rewards, while (as in the case of Iran) not paying any price, blowback-style, for decades, if at all. That was imperial power in the blaze of the noonday sun. These days, blowback for our imperial actions seems to arrive as if by high-speed rail (of which, by the way, the greatest power on the planet has yet to build a single mile).

It's been relatively easy, if you live in the United States, to notice little enough of all this and—at least until Donald Trump arrived, to the stunned fascination of the country not to speak of the rest of the planet—to imagine that we live in a peaceable land with most of its familiar markers still reassuringly in place. We still have elections, our tripartite form of government (as well as the other accouterments of a democracy), our reverence for our Constitution and the rights it endows us with, and so on. In truth, however, the American world is coming to bear ever less resemblance to the one we still claim as ours, or rather that older America looks increasingly like a hollowed-out shell within which something new and quite different has since been gestating.

Can anyone really doubt that representative democracy as it once existed has been eviscerated and is now—consider Congress exhibit A—in a state of advanced paralysis or that just about every aspect of the country's infrastructure is slowly fraying or crumbling with little being done about it? Can anyone doubt that the constitutional system—take war powers as a prime example or, for that matter, American civil liberties—has also been fraying? Can anyone doubt that the country's classic tripartite form of government—with a Supreme Court missing a member by choice of Congress and a national security state that mocks the law—is ever less checked-and-balanced and increasingly more than "tri"?

In the Vietnam era, people first began talking about an "imperial presidency." Today, in areas of overwhelming importance, the White House is, if anything, somewhat less imperial, but only because it's more in thrall to the ever-expanding national security state. Though that unofficial fourth branch of government is seldom seriously considered in descriptions of the ways in which our American world works and though it has no place in the Constitution, it is increasingly the first branch of government in Washington, the one before which all the others kneel.

There was, in what seemed like an endless election season, much discussion of Donald Trump's potential for "authoritarianism" (or incipient "fascism," or worse). It was a subject generally treated as if it were some tendency or property unique to the man who rode a Trump Tower escalator into the presidential race to the tune of Neil Young's "Rockin' in the Free World," or perhaps something from the 1930s that he carried around in his jacket pocket and that his enthusiastic white working-class followers were naturally drawn to and responsible for.

Few bothered to consider the ways in which the foundations of authoritarianism had already been laid in this society—and not by disaffected working-class white men either. Or what it meant to have a national security state and a massive military machine deeply embedded in our ruling city and our American world. Few thought about the no less than seventeen significant intelligence agencies that eat close to $70 billion annually, or the trillion dollars or more a year that disappears into our national security world, or what it means for that state-within-a-state, that shadow government, to become ever more powerful and autonomous in the name of American "safety," especially from "terrorism" (though terrorism actually represents the most microscopic of dangers for most Americans).

Amid all the charges leveled at Donald Trump, where did we see serious discussion of what it meant for the Pentagon's spy drones to be flying missions over the "homeland," or for "intelligence" agencies to be employing the kind of blanket surveillance of everyone's communications—from foreign leaders to peasants in Afghanistan to American citizens—that, technologically speaking, put the totalitarian regimes of the previous century to shame? Is there nothing of the authoritarian lurking in all this? Could that urge really be the property of The Donald and his followers alone?

The Greatest Show on Earth

In early May 2016, after a long, long run, the elephants of the Ringling Bros. and Barnum & Bailey Circus were ushered into retirement in Florida where they will finish their days aiding cancer research. The Greatest Show on Earth was done with its pachyderms. The same might be said about the Republicans after Donald Trump's version of a GOP convention. Many of them had also been sent, far less gracefully than those circus elephants, into a kind of enforced retirement (without even cancer research as an excuse).

Their former party remained in the none-too-gentle hands of the eternally aggrieved Trump, while the Democrats were left to happily chant "USA! USA!," march a barking retired four-star general and a former CIA director on stage to invoke the indispensable "greatness" of America, and otherwise exhibit the kind of super-patriotism and worship of the military usually associated with, no question about it, the GOP (whose delegates, meanwhile, spent their time chanting "lock her up!").

And that's just to take the tiniest of peeks at a passing moment in what continued to be, without the slightest doubt, the Greatest Show on Earth in 2016.

Untold billions of words were expended on this "election" and the outsized histories, flaws, and baggage Donald Trump and Hillary Clinton brought with them in their presidential run. Had there ever been this sort of coverage, hour after hour, day after day, night after night?

Has the *New York Times* ever featured stories about the same candidate and his cronies, two at a time, on its front page daily as it did when it highlighted the antics of The Donald? Were there ever so many "experts" of every stripe jawing away about a single subject on cable TV from the crack of dawn to the witching hour? Had such a mass of pundits ever churned out opinions by the hour? Had there ever been so many polls about the American people's electoral desires? And, of course, those polls were then covered, discussed, and analyzed endlessly. Years ago, Jonathan Schell suggested that we no longer had an election, but (thanks to those polls) "serial elections." Schell wrote that back in the Neolithic age, and we've come an awful long way since then. There were websites, after all, that seemed to do little more than produce mega-polls from all the polls spewing out.

And as for the completely self-referential nature of Election 2016: if ever there was an event that was about itself and focused only on itself, this was it. Donald Trump has taken possession of Twitter and his furious—in every sense, since he's the thinnest-skinned political figure ever—tweets rapidly pile up and are absorbed into "news" articles about the campaign that are, in turn, tweeted out for The Donald to potentially tweet about himself, in a Möbius strip of blather.

What We Can't Blame Donald Trump For

Despite all the analysis and those polls stumbling over each other to illuminate next to nothing, it seems there's something unsaid, something unpolled, something missing.

As the previous world of American politics melts and the electoral seas continue to rise, those of us in the coastal outlands of domestic politics find ourselves, like so many climate refugees, fleeing the tides of spectacle, insult, propaganda, and the rest. We're talking about a phenomenon that's engulfing us. We've been drowning in a sea of words and images called "Election 2016." We have no more accurate name for it, no real way to step back and describe the waters that we've been drowning in.

We can blame Donald Trump for many things in that bizarre season of political theater, but we can't blame him for the phenomenon itself. He may have been made for such a moment with his uncanny knack for turning himself into a never-ending news cycle of one, while scarfing up billions of dollars of free publicity, but he was a Johnny-come-lately to the process itself. After all, he wasn't one of the Supreme Court justices who, in their 2010 *Citizens United* decision, green-lighted the flooding of American politics with the dollars of the ultra-wealthy in the name of free speech and in amounts that boggle the imagination (even as that same court has gone ever easier on the definition of political "corruption"). As a certified tightwad, Trump wasn't the one who made it possible to more or less directly purchase a range of politicians and so ensure that we would have our first one-percent elections. Nor was he the one who made American politics into a perfect arena for a rogue billionaire with enough money (and chutzpah) to buy himself.

It's true that no political figure has ever had The Donald's TV sense. Still, before he was even a gleam in his own presidential eye, the owners of cable news and other TV outlets had already grasped that an election season extending from here to hell might morph into a cornucopia of profits. He wasn't the one who realized that such an ever-expanding campaign season would not only bring in billions of dollars in political ads (thanks again, Supreme Court for helping to loose super PACs on the world), but billions more from advertisers for prime spots in the ongoing media spectacle itself. He wasn't the one who realized that a cable news channel with a limited staff could put every ounce of energy, every talking head they had at their disposal, into such an election campaign, and in remarkable ways, solve endless problems for a year or more. This was all apparent by the 2012 election, as debates spread across the calendar, ad money poured in, and the yakking never stopped. Donald Trump didn't create this version of an eternal reality show; he just became its temporary host and Hillary Clinton his quick-to-learn apprentice.

And yet, one thing is clear: neither those Supreme Court justices, nor the owners of TV outlets, nor the pundits, politicians, and pollsters, nor any of the rest of the crew knew what exactly they were creating. Think of them as the American equivalent of the blind men and the elephant. In this riot of confusion that passed for an election, with one candidate who was a walking Ponzi scheme and the other who (with her husband) had shamelessly pocketed staggering sums from the financial and tech sectors, what were we to make of "our" strange new world? Certainly, this was no longer just an election campaign. It was more like a way of life and, despite all the debates (that garnered National Football League–sized audiences), it was also the Tao of confusion.

Missing in Action

Let's start with this: The spectacle of our moment is so overwhelming, dominating every screen of our lives and focused on just two outsized individuals in a country of 300 million-plus on a planet of billions, that it blocks our view of reality. Whatever Election 2016 may have been, it blotted out much of the rest of the world. The only story sure to break through such otherwise nonstop coverage was someone picking up an assault rifle, revving up a truck, getting his hands on a machete, building a bomb, declaring loyalty to ISIS (whatever his disturbed thoughts may have been thirty seconds earlier), and slaughtering as many people as he could in the United States or Europe. Far grimmer and more frequent slaughters in Iraq, Turkey, Afghanistan, and other such places have no similar value and are generally ignored.

Of course, such carnage, when it did break through the election frenzy, only fed the growth of the campaign. It's a reasonable suspicion that somewhere at the heart of Election 2016 lay a deepening sense of fear about American life that seems to exhibit itself openly only in relation to one of its lesser dangers (Islamic terrorism). Much as this election campaign offered a strife-riven playing field for two, it also seemed to minimize the actual strife and danger in our world by focusing so totally on ISIS and its lone wolf admirers in the Western world. It might, in that sense, be considered a strange propaganda exercise in the limits of reality.

Let's take, for instance, our wars. Yes, the decision to invade Iraq was discussed (and criticized) during the campaign, and the zeal of both presidential candidates and every other candidate in the primaries to defeat and destroy the Islamic State was indeed overwhelming. In addition, Trump has pointed to the lack of any military victories in all these years, and the disaster of Clinton's interventionist urge in Libya. In an obvious exercise of super-patriotic fervor of the sort that once would have been strange in this country and now has become second nature, both the Democratic and Republican national conventions trotted out retired generals and national security officials to lecture the American public like so many rabid drill sergeants. Then there were the usual rites, especially prominent at the Democratic convention, dedicated to the temple of the "fallen" in our wars, and endless obeisance to the "warriors" and the military generally. There was, as well, the prolonged Trumpian controversy over the family of one dead Muslim-American Marine. One of the two candidates made a habit of praising to the heavens "the world's greatest military" (and you know just which one she meant) while swearing fealty to our generals and admirals; the other has decried that military as a "disaster" area, a "depleted" force "in horrible shape." For both, this adds up to the same thing: yet more money and support for that force.

Here's the strange thing. Largely missing in action in Election 2016 has been any serious assessment of, or real debate about, the actual wars being fought by the US military, or what the national security state has or hasn't accomplished in these years. Such questions have been notably absent from campaign speeches and media appearances, as has been the massive destruction in Iraq or Syria; or what it's meant for the "world's greatest military" to unleash its air power from Afghanistan to Libya, send out its drones on assassination missions from Pakistan to Somalia, launch special operations raids across the Greater Middle East and Africa, occupy two countries, and have nothing to show for it but the spread of ever-more viral and brutal terror movements and the collapse or near collapse of many of the states in which it's fought these wars.

In 2009, Leon Panetta, then head of the CIA, talked up America's drone assassination campaign in Pakistan as "the only game in town" when it came to stopping al-Qaeda. Today, you could say that in Washington the only game in town is failure. Similarly, the American taxpayer pours nearly $70 billion annually into the seventeen major and various minor outfits in its vast "intelligence" apparatus, and yet, as shown by the recent coup in Turkey, that intelligence community seldom seems to have a clue about what's going on.

Failed intelligence and failed wars in an increasingly failed world is a formula for anxiety, even fear. But all of this has been absorbed into and deflected by the unparalleled bread-and-circus spectacle of Election 2016, which has become a kind of addictive habit for "the people." Even fear has been transformed into another form of entertainment. In the process, the electorate has been turned into so many spectators, playing their small parts in a demobilizing show of the first order.

And speaking about other realities that went MIA, you wouldn't know it from Election 2016 coverage, but much of the United States was sweltering under a "heat dome" the week of the Democratic National Convention. It wasn't a phrase that had previously been in popular use and yet almost the whole country was at that moment living through record or near-record summer temperatures in a year in which, globally, each of the first six months had broken all previous heat records (as, in fact, had the last eight months of 2015). Even pre-heat-dome conditions in the lower forty-eight had been setting records for warmth (and don't even ask about Alaska). It might almost look like a pattern.

Unfortunately, as the world careens toward "an environment never experienced before," according to the National Oceanic and Atmospheric Administration, one of the two parties to the American election spectacle continues to insist that climate change is a hoax. Its politicians are almost uniformly in thrall to Big Energy, and its presidential candidate topped the charts when it comes to climate denialism. ("The concept of global warming," he's claimed, "was created by and for the Chinese in order to make US manufacturing non-competitive.") Meanwhile, the other party, the one theoretically promoting much-needed responses to climate change, wasn't even willing to highlight the subject in prime time on any of the last three days of its convention.

In other words, the deepest, most unnerving realities of our world have, in essence, been missing in action in Election 2016.

The Shrinking Election Phenomenon

So, what was this spectacle of ours? Certainly, as a show it caught many of our fears, sweeping them up in its whirlwind and then burying them in unreality. Election season can rouse audiences to a fever pitch and seems to act like a Rorschach test in which you read whatever you're inclined to see into its most recent developments.

So much of American "democracy" and so many of the funds that we pony up to govern ourselves now go into strengthening the power of essentially anti-democratic structures: a military with a budget larger than those of the next seven or eight countries combined and the rest of a national security state of a size unimaginable in the pre–9/11 era. Each institution is now deeply embedded in Washington and each is at least as grotesque in its bloat as the 2016 election campaign itself. We're talking about structures that have remarkably little to do with self-governance or We the People (even though it's constantly drummed into our heads that both are there to protect us, the people). In these years, even as they have proven capable of winning next to nothing and detecting little, they've grown ever larger, more imperial, and powerful.

No matter. We're all under the heat dome now and when tens of millions of us troop to the polls, who knows what we're really doing anymore, except of course paving the way for the next super-spectacle of our political age, Election 2020. Count on it: speculation about the candidates for our next election will begin in the media within days after the results of this one are in. And it's a guarantee: there will be nothing like it. It will dazzle, entrance, amaze. It's going to be . . . the Greatest Show on Earth.

This Is Not about Donald Trump

It seems reasonable to conclude that never in history has the media covered a single human being as it has Donald Trump. For more than a year, he was the news cycle, essentially the only one, morning, noon, and night, day after day, week after week, month after month. His every word, phrase, move, insult, passing comment, off-the-cuff remark, claim, boast, brazen lie, shout, or shout-out has been ours as well. He's only been banished from the headlines and the screen for relatively brief periods, usually when Islamic terrorist groups or domestic "lone wolves" struck, as in San Bernardino, Paris, or Orlando, and, given his campaign, that worked no less well for his purposes than being the center of attention himself, as it will for his presidency. In this period, he's praised his secret plan to destroy ISIS and take Iraqi oil. He's thumped that "big, fat, beautiful wall" again and again. He's birthered a campaign to transport himself, improbably enough, into the Oval Office. He's fought it out with seventeen political rivals, including "lyin' Ted," "low-energy Jeb," Carly ("Look at that face! Would anyone vote for that?") Fiorina, "crooked Hillary," a Miss Universe ("Miss Piggy"), the "highly overrated" Megyn Kelly's menstrual cycle ("You could see there was blood coming out of her eyes, blood coming out of her wherever"), always Rosie O'Donnell ("a slob [with] a fat, ugly face"), and so many others. He's made veiled assassination threats; lauded the desire to punch someone in the face; talked about shooting "somebody" in "the middle of Fifth Avenue"; defended the size of his hands and his you-know-what; retweeted neo-Nazis and a quote from Mussolini; denounced the outsourcing of American manufacturing jobs and products while outsourcing his own jobs and products; excoriated immigrants and foreign labor while hiring the same; advertised the Trump brand in every way imaginable; had a bromance with Vladimir Putin; threatened to let nuclear weapons proliferate; complained bitterly about a rigged election, rigged debates, a rigged moderator, and a rigged microphone; swore that he and he alone was capable of again making America, and so the world, a place of the sort of greatness only he himself could match, and that's just to begin a list on the subject of The Donald.

In other words, thanks to the media attention he garners incessantly, he is the living embodiment of our American moment. No matter what you think of him, his has been a journey of a sort we've never seen before, a triumph of the first order. He's burnished his own brand; opened a new hotel on—yes—Pennsylvania Avenue (which he used his election run to promote and publicize); sold his products mercilessly; promoted his children; funneled dollars to his family and businesses; and in an unspoken alliance (pact, entente, détente) of the first order, kept the nightly news and the cable networks rolling in dough and in the spotlight (as long as they kept yakking about him), despite the fact that younger viewers were in flight to the universe of social media, streaming services, and their smartphones.

Thanks to the millions, billions, perhaps trillions of words expended on him by nonstop commentators, pundits, talking heads, retired generals and admirals, former intelligence chiefs, ex–Bush administration officials, and god-knows-who-else that have kept the cable channels churning with Trump on a nearly 24/7 basis, he and his remarkable ego and his now-familiar gestures—that jut-jawed look, that orange hair, that overly tanned face, that eternally raised voice—have become the wallpaper of our lives, something close to our reality. We've never seen anything like him or it, and yet, strange as the Trump phenomenon may be, if you think about it for a moment, you'll realize that there's also something eerily familiar about him, and not just because of *The Apprentice* and *Celebrity Apprentice*.

In a world where so many things deserve our attention and don't receive it, rest assured that this is not about Donald Trump. It really isn't.

In terms of any presidential candidate from George Washington to Barack Obama, Trump is little short of a freak of nature. There's really no one to compare him to (other, perhaps, than George Wallace). Sometimes his pitch about America—and a return to greatness—has a faintly Reaganesque quality (but without any of Ronald Reagan's sunniness or charm).

Still, as a phenomenon, Donald Trump couldn't be more American—as American, in fact, as a piece of McDonald's baked apple pie. What could be more American, after all, than his two major roles: salesman (or pitchman) and con artist? From P. T. Barnum (who, by the way, became the mayor of Bridgeport, Connecticut, late in life) to Willy Loman, protagonist of Arthur Miller's *Death of a Salesman*, selling has long been an iconic American way to go. A man who sells his life and brand as the ultimate American life and brand—what's not familiar about that?

As for being a con man, since at least Mark Twain (remember the Duke of Bridgewater and the Dauphin, who join Huck and Jim on their raft?) and Herman Melville (*The Confidence Man*), the charm of the huckster in American life can't be denied. It's something Donald Trump knows in his bones, even if all those pundits and commentators and pollsters (and, for that matter, Hillary Clinton's advisers) don't: Americans love a con man. Historically, we've often admired, if not identified with, someone intent on playing and successfully beating the system, whether at a confidence game or through criminal activity.

After the first presidential debate, when Trump essentially admitted that in some years he paid no taxes ("that makes me smart") and that he had played the tax system for everything it was worth, there was all that professional *tsk-tsk*ing and the prediction that such an admission would deeply disturb ordinary voters who pay up when the IRS comes knocking. Don't believe it for a second. Trump senses that with such statements he's deep in the Mississippi of American politics and that a surprising number of voters will admire him for it (whether they admit it or not). After all, he beat the system, even if they didn't.

The legendary Chicago crime boss of the 1920s, Al Capone, once told British journalist Claud Cockburn: "Listen, don't get the idea I'm one of those goddamn radicals. . . . Don't get the idea I'm knocking the American system. My rackets are run on strictly American lines. Capitalism, call it what you like, gives to each and every one of us a great opportunity if only we seize it with both hands and make the most of it." Indeed, Trump's "rackets" are similarly "run on strictly American lines." He's the Tony Soprano of casino capitalism and so couldn't be more American.

Yet there are aspects of his role that are so new they should startle us all. Begin with the fact that he's the first declinist candidate for president of our era. Put another way, he's the only politician in the country who refuses to engage in a ritual of affirmations of the United

States as the greatest, most exceptional, most indispensable nation of all time that possesses the "finest fighting force in the history of the world." Undoubtedly, that by-now-kneejerk urge to repeat such formulaic sentiments reflects creeping self-doubts about America's future imperial role and so has the quality of a magic mantra being used to ward off reality. After all, when a great power truly is at its height, as the United States was in my youth, no one feels the need to continually, defensively insist that it's so.

In relation to his Republican rivals in the primaries, and Hillary Clinton in the general election, Donald Trump stands alone in accepting and highlighting what increasing numbers of Americans, especially white Americans, have evidently come to feel: that this country is in decline, its greatness a thing of the past, or, as pollsters like to put it, that America is no longer "heading in the right direction" but is now "on the wrong track." In this way, he has mainlined into a deep, economically induced mindset, especially among white working-class men facing a situation in which so many good jobs have headed elsewhere, that the world has turned sour.

A significant part of the white working class, at least, feels as if, whether economically or psychologically, its back is up against the wall and there's nowhere left to go. Under such circumstances, many of these voters have evidently decided that they're ready to send a loose cannon into the White House; they're willing, that is, to take a chance on the roof collapsing, even if it collapses on them.

That is the new and unrecognizable role that Donald Trump has filled. It's hard to recall another example of it in our recent past. The Donald represents, as a friend of mine likes to say, the suicide bomber in us all. And voting for him, among other things, will be an act of nihilism, a mood that fits well with our period of imperial decline.

This is not about Donald Trump. It's about us.

The Comb-Over in the Mirror

So much of this is about money, ratings, and the coffers of those who own TV networks. Gluing eyeballs to screens (and ads) is, of course, the real news about the news. CBS CEO Leslie Moonves couldn't have

been blunter on how the present system works. At a Morgan Stan-
ley investors' conference, speaking of the Trump campaign, Moonves
said, "It may not be good for America, but it's damn good for CBS."
And then he added: "The money's rolling in and this is fun. I've never
seen anything like this, and this [is] going to be a very good year for us.
Sorry. It's a terrible thing to say. But, bring it on, Donald. Keep going."

We know, roughly speaking, what Moonves and his ilk make of
the frenetic onscreen world their employees present us with—a world
of relative inconsequence that is often, at one and the same moment,
horrifying, fascinating, stupefying, shocking, enervating, saddening,
and even, if you happen to like Donald or Ted or Hillary or Bernie,
sometimes uplifting or hopeful.

What are we to make of this spectacle? The most obvious thing
that can be said is that it leaves us painfully unprepared to face, or
grasp, or begin to deal with the world as it actually is. What's left out of
this coverage? Well, more or less everything that truly matters much
of the time: any large, generally unphotogenic process, for instance,
like the crumbling of America's infrastructure (unless cameras can
fortuitously be present to zoom in on a bridge collapsing or a natural
gas pipeline in the process of blowing up in a neighborhood—all so
much more likely in an age in which no imaginable situation lacks
its amateur videographer); poverty (who the hell cares?); the growing
inequality gap locally or globally; almost anything that happens in the
places where most of the people on this planet actually live (Asia and
Africa); the rise of the national security state and of militarism in an
era of permanent war and permanent (in)security in the "homeland";
and climate change.

The menu of the news, as presently defined, lowers your chance of
understanding the world. It is, however, likely to raise your blood pressure and your sense of fear in a world in which there is plenty of reason
to be afraid, but seldom of what's on screen. In a sense, at its best, what
the all-day obsession that's still called "the news" really provides is the
kind of rush that we might normally associate with a drug or other
addiction rather than with reportage or analysis.

The news increasingly does several things:

1. It creates its own heightened, insular world to replace the world we actually live in.

2. At its most effective, it's like a recurrent floodtide washing over you.

3. It has an obsessional quality, with single stories engulfing everything else, inducing a deeply skewed view of the world, no matter what event or events are being followed. Who can doubt that the Internet, social media, email, and the rest of the package are the signature addictive activities of our age?

The "news" is a key part of this addictive package. In a sense, in an age of electronic obsession, onscreen news purveyors like Moonves may have little choice but to make it so—it's that or, assumedly, watch your cable network or key news programs die a grim financial death. Donald Trump is certainly *sui generis* and regularly admired for the deft way he plays the news and the media to his advantage. He's less commonly thought of as the creature of the news and the media: in a sense, he's their ultimate creation of this moment, the current top-of-the-line drug on offer. If he's also the ultimate narcissist without filters, then perhaps what we still call "the news" is itself a new form of narcissism.

Crimes of the Trump Era (a Preview)

While becoming president, Donald Trump emerged as a media phenomenon of a sort we've never seen before.

First, it was those billions of dollars in advertising the media forked over gratis during the race for the Republican nomination by focusing on whatever he did, said, or tweeted, day after day. By the time he hit the campaign trail against Hillary Clinton, he was the ultimate audience magnet and the cameras and reporters were fused to him, so coverage only ballooned, as it did again during the transition months leading up to his inauguration. Now, Trump's presidency is the story of the second—each second of every day.

Never in the history of the media has a single figure—one human being—been able to focus the "news" in this way, making himself

the essence of all reporting. One man's narcissism gains new meaning when inflated to a societal level. Yes, while at certain moments in
history—the assassination of John F. Kennedy, O. J. Simpson's white
Bronco chase, the 9/11 attacks—a single event or personality has over-
whelmed everything else and taken the news by storm, never has one
person been able to do this through thick and thicker, through moments of actual news and moments when nothing whatsoever is happening to him.

As an example, consider the *New York Times*. At the moment,
Trump or people and events related to him monopolize its front page
in a way that's beyond rare. He now regularly sweeps up four or five of
its six or so front-page headlines daily, and a staggering six to ten full,
often six-column, pages of news coverage inside—and that's not even
counting the editorial and op-ed pages, which these days are a riot of
Trumpery. From early morning till late at night, we face an avalanche
of Trumpified news and features.

Yet in the never-ending weeks after his election, Donald Trump
did the seemingly impossible: he stirred protest on a global scale;
sparked animosity, if not enmity, and nationalism from Mexico to
Iraq, England to China; briefly united Mexico behind one of the least
popular presidents in its history; insulted the Australian prime minister, alienating America's closest ally in Asia; and that's just to begin a
list of the president's earliest "accomplishments."

So how can we put any of this in context while drowning in the
moment? Perhaps one way to start would be by trying to look past the
all-enveloping "news" of yesterday, today, and tomorrow.

Were you to do so, you might conclude that, despite all the sound
and the fury, almost nothing had yet actually happened. I know that's
hard to believe under the circumstances, but the age of Trump—or indeed, the damage of Trump—had essentially yet to begin (though tell
that to the Iraqis, Iranians, and others caught in mid-air flights, cuffed
on the ground, and in some cases sent back into a hell on Earth). Still,
crises? The media is already talking about constitutional ones, but believe me, you ain't seen nothin' yet. Conflicts of interest? So far, grim
as the news may look, there's hardly been a hint of what's sure to come.
And crimes against the country? They've hardly begun.

It's true that Trump's national security appointments, from the Pentagon and the CIA to the Department of Homeland Security and the National Security Council, are largely in place, even if reportedly already in a state of flux as National Security Advisor Michael Flynn seems to be losing his grip on the new president. Otherwise, few of his cabinet appointments are truly functional yet. That set of billionaires and multimillionaires are either barely confirmed or not yet so. They haven't even begun to preside over departments filled with staffs that instantly seem to be in chaos, living in fear, or moving into a mood of resistance.

This means that what Bill Moyers has already termed the "demolition derby" of the Trump era hasn't yet really begun, despite a hiring freeze on the non-national-security-state part of the government. Or put another way, if the last two weeks were news, let's just wait for the wealthiest cabinet in our history to settle in, a true crew of predatory capitalists, including a commerce secretary nicknamed "the king of bankruptcy" for his skills in buying up wrecked companies at staggering profits; a Treasury secretary dubbed the "foreclosure king" of California for evicting thousands of homeowners (including active-duty military families) from distressed properties he and his partners picked up in the wake of the 2008 financial meltdown; and a head of the State Department who only recently led ExxonMobil in its global depredations.

As a crew, they and their compatriots are primed to either dismantle the agencies they'll run or shred their missions. That includes head of the Environmental Protection Agency Scott Pruitt, a man long in the pay of Big Energy, who seems determined to reduce the EPA to a place that protects us from nothing; and a fast-food king who, as the prospective new labor secretary, is against the minimum wage and would love to replace workers with machines.

And let's not forget the White House, now that it's a family operation—a combination of a real-estate-based global branding outfit (the Trumps) and a real estate empire (son-in-law Jared Kushner). It's obvious that decisions made in the White House, but also in government offices in foreign capitals, on the streets of foreign cities, and even among jihadists, will affect the fortunes of those two families. As patriarch, Donald J. will, of course, rule the Oval Office; his son-in-law will be down the hall somewhere, with constant access to him; and his daughter Ivanka is to have an as-yet-unannounced role in her father's administration.

FOUR

The Making of a Pariah Nation

From healthcare and tax policy to environmental protections, this will undoubtedly be a government of the looters, by the looters, and for the looters, and a Congress of the same.

In such a leave-no-billionaires-behind era, forget the past swamps of Washington (which wasn't really built on swampland) that Trump promises to drain. The government of Donald J. Trump seems slated to produce an American swamp of swamps and, somewhere down the line, will surely give new meaning to the phrase "conflict of interest."

From a government of one-percent looters, what can we expect but to be looted and to experience crimes of every sort? Still, whatever those may turn out to be, in the end they will just be the usual crimes of human history. In them, there will be little new, except perhaps in their extremity in the United States. They will cause pain, of course— as well as gain for the few—but sooner or later such crimes and those who commit them will pass from the scene and in the course of history be largely forgotten.

Of only one future crime will that not be true. As a result, it's likely to prove the most unforgivable of them all and those who help in its commission will, without a doubt, be the greatest criminals of all time. Think of them as terrarists and their set of acts as, in sum, terracide. If there's a single figure in the Trump administration who embodies the essence of this, it is, of course, former ExxonMobil CEO and present secretary of state Rex Tillerson. His former company has a grim history not just of exploiting fossil fuels come (literally) hell or high water, but of suppressing information about the harm they've done via greenhouse gas emissions that heat the atmosphere and the Earth's waters, while funding climate denialism; of, in short, destroying the planet in an eternal search for record profits.

Now, he joins an administration whose president once termed climate change a "Chinese hoax," and who has, with striking determination, appointed first to his transition team and then to his government an unparalleled crew of climate change deniers and so-called climate skeptics. They, and largely only they, are taking key positions in every department or agency of government in any way connected with fossil fuels or the environment. Among Trump's first acts was to green-light two much-disputed pipelines: one slated to transport the carbon-dirtiest of oil products, Canadian tar sands, from Alberta to the Gulf Coast; the other to encourage the frackers of the Bakken shale oil fields of North Dakota to keep up the good work. In his yearning to return us to a 1950s America, President Trump has promised a new age of fossil fuel exploitation. He's evidently ready to leave the Paris climate agreement in the trash heap of history and toss aside support for the development of alternative energy systems as well. In the process—and "irony" is too weak a word for this—he will potentially cede a monster job-creation machine to the Chinese, the Germans, and others.

Call it perfect scheduling, but just two days before his inauguration—two days, that is, before the White House website would be purged of all references to climate change—both the National Oceanic and Atmospheric Administration and the National Aeronautics and Space Administration (NASA)—each undoubtedly soon to be scrubbed clean by Trump's climate deniers—announced that, in 2016, the planet's temperature had broken all heat records for an unprecedented third year in a row. (This means that sixteen out of the top seventeen hottest years on record occurred in the twenty-first century.) From 2013 to 2016, according to NASA, the planet warmed by well over a half-degree Fahrenheit, "the largest temperature increase over a three-year period in the NASA record."

In 2016, as the *Guardian* reported, "North America saw its highest number of storms and floods in over four decades. Globally, we saw over one and a half times more extreme weather catastrophes . . . than the average over the past thirty years. Global sea ice cover plunged to a record low as well." And that's just to start a list. This is no longer terribly complicated. It's not debatable science. It's our reality and there can be no question that a world of ever-more extreme weather events, rising sea levels, lengthening mega-droughts (as well as massive rainfalls), along with heat and more heat, is what the future holds for our children and grandchildren. Barring stunning advances in alternative energy technologies or other surprises, this, again, is too obvious to doubt.

So those, including our new president and his administration, who are focused on suppressing both scientific knowledge about climate change and any attempt to mitigate the phenomenon, or who, like Rex Tillerson's former colleagues at the big energy companies, prefer to suppress basic information in the name of fossil fuel production and personal enrichment, will be committing the most unforgivable of crimes against humanity.

As a group, they will be taking the US, the world's second-largest greenhouse gas emitter, out of the climate change sweepstakes for years to come and helping ensure that the welcoming planet on which humanity has so long existed will be something so much grimmer in the future. In this moment's endless flurry of "news" about Donald Trump, this—the most basic news of all—has, of course, been lost in the hubbub. And yet, unlike any other set of actions they could engage in (except perhaps nuclear war), this is truly the definition of forever news. Climate change, after all, operates on a different time scale than we do, being part of planetary history, and so may prove human history's deal breaker.

Applying Hard Power to a Failing World

As we watch, it seems almost possible to see President Trump, in real time, tweet by tweet, speech by speech, sword dance by sword dance, intervention by intervention, act by act, in the process of dismantling the system of global power—of "soft power," in particular, and of alliances of every sort—by which the United States made its will felt, made itself a truly global hegemon. Whether his "America First" policies are aimed at creating a future order of autocrats, or petro-states, or are nothing more than the expression of his own libidinous urges and secret hatreds, Trump may already be succeeding in taking down the world order in record fashion.

Despite the mainstream pieties of the moment about the nature of the system Donald Trump appears to be dismantling in Europe and elsewhere, that system was anything but particularly "liberal" or peaceable. Wars, invasions, occupations, the undermining or overthrow of governments, brutal acts and conflicts of every sort succeeded one another in the years of American glory. Past administrations in Washington had a notorious weakness for autocrats, just as Donald Trump does today. They regularly had less than no respect for democracy if, from Iran to Guatemala to Chile, the will of the people seemed to stand in Washington's way. (It is, as Vladimir Putin has been only too happy to point out of late, an irony of our moment that the country that has undermined or overthrown or meddled in more electoral systems than any other is in a total snit over the possibility that one of its own elections was tampered with.) To enforce their global system, Americans never shied away from torture, black sites, death squads, assassinations, and other grim practices. In those years, the United States planted its military on close to one thousand overseas military bases, garrisoning the planet as no other country ever had.

Nonetheless, the canceling of the Trans Pacific Partnership trade deal, the withdrawal from the Paris Agreement, threats against NAFTA, the undermining of NATO, the promise of protective tariffs on foreign goods (and the possible trade wars that might go with them) could go a long way toward dismantling the American global system of soft power and economic dominance as it has existed in these last decades. If such acts and others like them prove effective in the years to come, they will leave only one kind of power in the American global quiver: hard military power and its handmaiden, the kind of covert power Washington, through the CIA in particular, has long specialized in. If America's alliances crack open and its soft power becomes too angry or edgy to pass for dominant power anymore, its massive machinery of destruction will still remain, including its vast nuclear arsenal.

Given the last fifteen years of history, it's not hard to imagine what's likely to result from the further elevation of military power: disaster. This is especially true because Donald Trump has appointed to key positions in his administration a crew of generals who spent the last decade and a half fighting America's catastrophic wars in the Greater Middle East. They are not only notoriously incapable of thinking outside the box about the application of military power, but faced with failed wars and failing states, spreading terror movements and a growing refugee crisis across that crucial region, they can evidently only imagine one solution to just about any problem: more of the same. More troops, more mini-surges, more military trainers and advisers, more air strikes, more drone strikes . . . more.

After a decade and a half of such thinking we already know perfectly well where this ends: in further failure, more chaos and suffering, but above all in an inability of the United States to effectively apply its hard power anywhere in any way that doesn't make matters worse. Since, in addition, the Trump administration is filled with Iranophobes, including a president who has recently fused himself to the Saudi royal family in an attempt to further isolate and undermine Iran, the possibility that a military-first version of American foreign policy will spread further is only growing.

Such "more" thinking is typical as well of much of the rest of the cast of characters now in key positions in the Trump administration. Take the CIA, for instance. Under its new director, Mike Pompeo (distinctly a "more" kind of guy and an Iranophobe of the first order), two key positions have reportedly been filled: a new chief of counterterrorism and a new head of Iran operations (identified as Michael D'Andrea, an Agency hardliner with the nickname "the Dark Prince"). Here's how Matthew Rosenberg and Adam Goldman of the *New York Times* described their similar approaches to their jobs (my emphasis added):

> Mr. D'Andrea's new role is one of a number of moves inside the spy agency that signal *a more muscular approach* to covert operations under the leadership of Mike Pompeo, the conservative Republican and former congressman, the officials said. The agency also recently named a new chief of counterterrorism, who has begun *pushing for greater latitude to strike militants.*

In other words, more!

Rest assured of one thing, whatever Donald Trump accomplishes in the way of dismantling America's version of soft power, "his" generals and intelligence operatives will handle the hard power part of the equation just as "ably."

The First American Laster?

If a Trump presidency achieves a record for the ages when it comes to facilitating the precipitous decline of the American global system, little as The Donald ever cares to share credit for anything, he will undoubtedly have to share the glory. It's true that while kings, emperors, and autocrats, the top dogs of any moment, prefer to take all the credit for the "records" set in their time, when we look back, it's likely that President Trump will be seen as having given a tottering system that necessary push. It will undoubtedly be clear enough by then that the United States, seemingly at the height of any power's power in 1991 when the Soviet Union disappeared, began heading for the exits soon thereafter, still enwreathed in self-congratulation and triumphalism.

Had this not been so, Donald Trump would never have won the 2016 election. It wasn't he, after all, who gave the American heartland an increasingly Third World feel. It wasn't he who spent those trillions of dollars so disastrously on invasions and occupations, dead-end wars, drone strikes and special ops raids, reconstruction and deconstruction in a never-ending Global War on Terror that today looks more like a war for the spread of terror. It wasn't he who created the growing inequality gap in this country or produced all those billionaires amid a population that increasingly felt left in the lurch. It wasn't he who hiked college tuitions or increased the debt levels of the young or set roads and bridges to crumbling and created the conditions for crumbling airports.

Was 11/8 a New 9/11?

For decades, Washington had a habit of using the Central Intelligence Agency to deep-six foreign governments of the people, by the people, and for the people that weren't to its taste, replacing them with governments of the—take your pick: military junta, shah, autocrat, dictator— across the planet.

There was the infamous 1953 CIA- and British-organized coup that toppled the democratic Iranian government of Mohammad Mosaddegh and put the shah (and his secret police, the SAVAK) in power. There was the 1954 CIA coup against the government of Jacobo Arbenz in Guatemala that installed the military dictatorship of Carlos Castillo Armas; there was the CIA's move to make Ngo Dinh Diem the head of South Vietnam, also in 1954. In 1961, there was the CIA-Belgian plot to assassinate the Congo's first elected prime minister, Patrice Lumumba, that led, in the end, to the military dictatorship of Mobutu Sese Seko; in 1964, the CIA-backed military coup in Brazil that overthrew elected president João Goulart and brought to power a military junta; and, of course, the first 9/11 (September 11, 1973) when the democratically elected socialist president of Chile, Salvador Allende, was overthrown and killed in a US-backed military coup.

In this way, Washington repeatedly worked its will as the leader of what was then called "the Free World." Although such operations were carried out on the sly, when they were revealed, Americans, proud of their own democratic traditions, generally remained unfazed by what the CIA had done to democracies (and other kinds of governments) abroad in their name. If Washington repeatedly empowered regimes of a sort Americans would have found unacceptable for ourselves, it wasn't something that most of us spent a whole lot of time fretting about in the context of the Cold War.

At least those acts remained largely covert, undoubtedly reflecting a sense that this wasn't the sort of thing you should shamelessly broadcast in the light of day. In the early years of the twenty-first century, however, a new mindset emerged. In the wake of the 9/11 attacks, "regime change" became the phrase *du jour*. As a course of action, there was no longer any reason to be covert. Instead, the process was debated openly and carried out in the full glare of media attention.

No longer would Washington set the CIA plotting in the shadows to rid it of detested governments and put in their place more malleable client states. Instead, as the "sole superpower" of Planet Earth, with a military believed to be beyond compare or challenge, the Bush administration claimed the right to dislodge governments it disdained directly, bluntly, and openly with the straightforward use of military force. Later, the Obama administration would take the same tack under the rubric of "humanitarian intervention" or "R2P" ("responsibility to protect"). In this sense, regime change and R2P would become shorthand for Washington's right to topple governments in the full light of day by cruise missile, drone, and Apache helicopter, not to mention troops, if needed. (Saddam Hussein's Iraq would, of course, be exhibit A in this process and Muammar Gaddafi's Libya, exhibit B.)

With this history in mind, a question occurred to me: In 2016, did the American people leave the CIA in a ditch and do to themselves what the Agency (and more recently the US military) had done to others? In the strangest election of our lifetimes, have we just seen something like a slow-motion democratic coup d'état or some form of domestic regime change?

Only time will tell, but one sign of that possibility: for the first time, part of the national security state directly intervened in an American election. In this case, not the CIA, but our leading domestic investigative outfit, the FBI. As we now know, fulminating and plotting had been ongoing inside it against one of the two candidates for president before its director, James Comey, openly, even brazenly, entered the fray with eleven days to go. He did so on grounds that, even at the time, seemed shaky at best, if not simply bogus, and ran against firm department traditions of conduct for such election periods. In the process, his intervention may indeed have changed the trajectory of the election—an experience commonplace in the rest of the world, but a unique moment in this country.

Donald Trump's administration, now filling up with racists, Islamophobes, Iranophobes, and assorted fellow billionaires, already has the feel of an increasingly militarized, autocratic government, favoring short-tempered, militaristic white guys who don't take criticism lightly or react to speed bumps well. In addition, they will find themselves with immense repressive powers of every sort at their fingertips, powers ranging from torture to surveillance that were institutionalized in remarkable ways in the post–9/11 years, powers which some of them are clearly eager to test out.

History's Deal Breaker?

On September 12, 2001, you would have been hard put to guess just how the shock of the attacks of the previous day would play out in the United States and the world, so perhaps it's idle to speculate on what the events of 11/8/16, that fateful election day, will lead to in the years to come. Prediction's a dicey business in the best of times, and the future ordinarily is a black hole. But one thing does seem likely amid the murk: with the generals (and other officials) who ran America's failed wars these last years dominating the national security structure of a future Trump administration, our empire of chaos (including, perhaps, regime change) will indeed have come home. It's reasonable to think of the victory of Donald Trump and his brand of right-wing corporatist or billionaire populism and of the rising tide of white racism that has accompanied it as a 9/11–style shock to the body politic, even if it proves a slo-mo version of the original event.

As with 9/11, a long, blowback-ridden history preceded 11/8 and Donald Trump's triumph. That history included the institutionalization of permanent war as a way of life in Washington; the growing independent power and preeminence of the national security state and the accompanying growth and institutionalization of the most oppressive powers of that state, including intrusive surveillance of almost every imaginable sort; the return from distant battlefields of the technology

and mindset of permanent war; and the technological ability to assassinate whomever the White House chooses to kill (American citizens
included) in distant lands. And in terms of blowback, domestically
we must include the results of the Supreme Court's *Citizens United*
decision of 2010, which helped release staggering amounts of corporate and one-percenter funds from the engorged top of an increasingly
unequal society into the political system (without which a billionaire
president with a cabinet of billionaires and multimillionaires would
have been inconceivable).

In a moment that, in so many senses, is filling with extremism
and in which the all-American jihadists of the national security state
are clearly going to be riding high, it's at least possible that Election
2016 will prove to have been the equivalent of a slow-motion coup in
America. Donald Trump, like right-wing populists before him, has a
temperament that could lend itself not only to demagoguery, but to an
American version of authoritarianism, especially since, in recent years,
with a loss of rights and the strengthening of government powers, the
country has already moved in an autocratic direction, even if that's
been a little noted reality so far.

Whatever may have been ushered in with the events of 11/8, one
thing is increasingly certain about the country that Donald Trump
will govern. The most dangerous nation on the planet will now be ours.
Led by a man who knows remarkably little, other than how to ma-
nipulate the media (on which he's a natural-born genius) and, at least
in part, by the frustrated generals from America's war on terror, the
United States is likely to be more extreme, belligerent, irrational, filled
with manias, and heavily armed, its military funded to even greater
levels no other country could come close to, and with staggering powers to intervene, interfere, and repress worldwide.

It's not a pretty picture. And yet it's just a lead-in to what, undoubtedly, should be considered the ultimate question in Donald Trump's
America: With both the CIA's coup-making and the military's regime-change traditions in mind, could the United States also overthrow
a planet? If, as the head of what's already the world's second-largest
greenhouse gas emitter, Trump carries out the future energy policies
he promised during the election campaign—climate-science funding

torn up, climate agreements denounced or ignored, alternative energy development downplayed, pipelines green-lighted, fracking and other forms of fossil fuel extraction further encouraged, and the United States fully reimagined as the Saudi Arabia of North America—he will, in effect, be launching a regime-change action against Planet Earth.

All the rest of what a Trump administration might do, including ushering in a period of American autocracy, would be just part and parcel of human history. Autocracies come and go. Autocrats rise and die. Rebellions break out and fail. Democracies work and then don't. Climate change is, however, none of that. It may be part of planetary history, but not of human history. What the Trump administration does in the years to come could prove a grim period to live through but a passing matter, at least when compared to the possible full-scale destabilization of life on Earth and of history as we've known it these last thousands of years.

This would, of course, put 9/11 in the shade. The election victory of 11/8 might ultimately prove the shock of a lifetime, of any lifetime, for eons to come. That's the danger we've faced since 11/8, and make no mistake, it could be devastating.

Assassin-in-Chief

Since at least Dwight Eisenhower, American presidents have been in the camp of the assassins. With Eisenhower, it was the CIA's plot against Congolese prime minister Patrice Lumumba; with John Kennedy (and his brother, Attorney General Robert Kennedy), it was attempts to assassinate Cuba's Fidel Castro; with Richard Nixon (and his secretary of state Henry Kissinger), it was the killing of Chilean president Salvador Allende in a US-backed military coup.

In 1976, in the wake of Watergate, President Gerald Ford outlawed political assassination by executive order, a ban reaffirmed by subsequent presidents (although Ronald Reagan did direct Air Force planes to bomb Libyan autocrat Muammar Gaddafi's home). As this new century began, however, the sexiest high-tech killer around, the appropriately named Predator drone, would be armed with Hellfire missiles and sent into action in the war on terror, creating the possibility of presidential assassinations on a scale never before imagined in a Terminator version of our world.

At the behest of two presidents, George W. Bush and Barack Obama, a fleet of such robotic assassins would enter historically unique terrain as global hunter-killers outside official American war zones. They and their successors, Reaper drones (as in the Grim Reaper), would be dispatched on mass assassination sprees that have yet to end and that were largely organized in the White House itself, based on a regularly updated, presidentially approved "kill list."

In this way, the president, his aides, and his advisers have become judge, jury, and executioner for "terror suspects" (though often enough for any man, woman, or child who happened to be in the vicinity as well) halfway around the world. In the process, the commander-in-chief became a permanent assassin-in-chief. Now, presidents are tasked with overseeing the elimination of hundreds of people in other lands with a sense of "legality" granted them in secret memos by the lawyers of their own Justice Department.

So when it comes to assassinations, we were already on dark terrain before Donald Trump ever thought about running for president. Little noticed by anyone, he may already be developing the potential for a new style of presidential assassination—not in distant lands but right here at home. Start with his remarkable tweeting skills and the staggering thirty-nine million followers of whatever he tweets, among them numerous members of what's politely referred to as the alt-right.

Indeed, Trump is already a sort of Twitter hit man. Certainly, his power to lash out in 140 characters is no small thing. On December 12, 2016, for instance, he suddenly tweeted a criticism of arms-maker Lockheed Martin for producing the most expensive weapons system in history, the F-35 fighter jet: "The F-35 program and cost is out of control. Billions of dollars can and will be saved on military (and other) purchases after January 20th." The company's stock value promptly took a $4 billion hit.

He also seems to have been irritated by a *Chicago Tribune* column focused on Boeing CEO Dennis Muilenburg's criticisms of his comments on international trade and China, where that company does significant business. Muilenburg suggested, mildly enough, that the president "back off from the 2016 anti-trade rhetoric and perceived threats to punish other countries with higher tariffs or fees." In response, The Donald promptly took out after the company, calling for the cancellation of a Boeing contract for a new high-tech version of Air Force One. ("Boeing is building a brand new 747 Air Force One for future presidents, but costs are out of control, more than $4 billion. Cancel order!") That company's stock took a similar hit.

But giant military-industrial corporations can defend themselves. When it comes to regular citizens, it's another matter. Take Chuck Jones, president of an Indiana United Steelworkers local. He disputed Trump on how many jobs the president-elect had saved at Carrier Corporation. Significantly less, he insisted (quite accurately), than Trump claimed. That clearly bruised the president-elect's giant but remarkably fragile ego. Before he knew what hit him, Jones found himself the object of a typical Trumpian Twitter barrage. ("Chuck Jones, who is President of United Steelworkers 1999, has done a terrible job representing workers. No wonder companies flee country!") The next thing he knew, abusive and threatening calls were pouring in—things like, "We're coming for you" or, as Jones explained it, "Nothing that says they're gonna kill me, but, you know, you better keep your eye on your kids. We know what car you drive. Things along those lines."

In October 2015, Lauren Batchelder, an eighteen-year-old college student, had a similar experience after getting up at a campaign event and telling Trump that he was no "friend to women." The candidate promptly went on the Twitter attack, labeling her "arrogant," and the next thing she knew, as the *Washington Post* described it, "her phone began ringing with callers leaving threatening messages that were often sexual in nature. Her Facebook and email inboxes filled with similar messages. As her addresses circulated on social media and her photo flashed on the news, she fled home to hide."

On this basis, it's not hard to make a prediction. One of these days in Trump's presidency, he will strike out by tweet at a private citizen ("Sad!") who got under his skin. In response, some unhinged member of what might be thought of as his future alt-drone force will pick up a gun (of which so many more will be so much closer at hand in the NRA-ascendant age of Trump). Then, in the fashion of the person who decided to "self-investigate" a pizza shop in Washington that—thank you, "fake news"—was supposed to be the center of a Hillary Clinton child-sex-slave ring, he will go self-investigate in person and armed. In "Pizzagate," the fellow fired his assault rifle harmlessly in that restaurant, whose owner had already received more than his share of abusive phone messages and death threats. It's easy enough to imagine, however, quite another result of such an event in which Donald Trump will have given "assassination by drone" a new meaning. And should that happen, what will be the consequences of the first presidential Twitter "hit" job in our history?

Don't forget that thanks to George W. Bush and Barack Obama, Trump will also have all those CIA drones to use as he wishes, to knock off whomever he chooses halfway across the planet. But as a potential Twitter assassin, rousing his alt-drones to the attack, he would achieve quite another kind of American first.

It Can Happen Here (In Fact, It Did!)

I simply couldn't accept that Donald Trump had won. Not him. Not in this country. Not possible. Not in a million years.

Mind you, during the campaign I had written about Trump repeatedly, always leaving open the possibility that, in the disturbed (and disturbing) America of 2016, he could indeed beat Hillary Clinton. That was a thought I lost when, in the final few weeks of the campaign, like so many others, I got hooked on the polls and the pundits who went with them. (Doh!)

In the wake of the election, however, it wasn't shock based on pollsters' errors that got to me. It was something else that only slowly dawned on me. Somewhere deep inside, I simply didn't believe that, of all countries on this planet, the United States could elect a narcissistic, celeb billionaire who was also, in the style of Italy's Silvio Berlusconi, a right-wing "populist" and incipient autocrat.

Post-election, here was the shock for me: it turned out that like Trump, I, too, was an American exceptionalist. I deeply believed that our country was simply too special for The Donald, and so his victory sent me on an unexpected journey back into the world of my youth, back into the 1950s and early 1960s when (despite the Soviet Union) the United States really did stand alone on the planet in so many ways. Of course, in those years, no one had to say such things—all those greatests, exceptionals, and indispensables were then dispensable.

In those bedrock years of American power and strength and wealth and drive and dynamism (and McCarthyism, and segregation, and racism, and smog, and . . .), the very years that Donald Trump now yearns to bring us back to, I took in that feeling of our specialness in ways too deep to grasp. Which was why, decades later, when I least expected it, I couldn't shake the feeling that it couldn't happen here. In actuality, the rise to power of Trumpian figures—Rodrigo Duterte in the Philippines, Viktor Orbán in Hungary, Recep Tayyip Erdoğan in Turkey, Vladimir Putin in Russia—has been a dime-a-dozen event elsewhere and now looks to be a global trend.

So how *did* it happen here?

Let's face it: Donald Trump was no freak of nature. He only arrived on the scene and took the Electoral College (if not the popular vote) because our American world had been prepared for him in so many ways. At least five major shifts in American life and politics helped lay the groundwork for the rise of Trumpism:

THE COMING OF A ONE-PERCENT ECONOMY
AND THE ONE-PERCENT POLITICS THAT GOES WITH IT

A singular reality of the twenty-first century is the way inequality has become embedded in American life, and how so much money was swept ever upwards into the coffers of one-percent profiteers. Meanwhile, a yawning gap grew between the basic salaries of CEOs and those of ordinary workers. In these years, as I'm hardly the first to point out, the country entered a new gilded age. In other words, it was already a Mar-a-Lago moment before The Donald threw his hair into the ring.

Without the arrival of casino capitalism on a massive scale (at which The Donald himself proved something of a bust), Trumpism would have been inconceivable. And if, in its *Citizens United* decision of 2010, the Supreme Court hadn't thrown open the political doors quite so welcomingly to that one-percent crew, how likely was it that a billionaire celebrity would have run for president or become a favorite among the white working class?

Perhaps Donald Trump deserves credit for exposing the true face of twenty-first-century American plutocracy in Washington by selecting mainly billionaires and multimillionaires to head the various departments and agencies of his government. After all, doesn't it seem reasonable that a one-percent economy, a one-percent society, and a one-percent politics should produce a one-percent government? Think of what Trump has so visibly done as American democracy's version of truth in advertising. And of course, if billionaires hadn't multiplied like rabbits in this era, he wouldn't have had the pool of plutocrats to choose from.

Something similar might be said of his choice of so many retired generals and other figures with significant military backgrounds (ranging from West Point graduates to a former Navy SEAL) for key "civilian" positions in his government—a truth-in-advertising moment leading directly to the second shift in American society.

THE COMING OF PERMANENT WAR
AND AN EVER-MORE MILITARIZED STATE AND SOCIETY

Can there be any question that, in the years since 9/11, what was originally called the "Global War on Terror" has become a permanent war across the Greater Middle East and Africa (with collateral damage from Europe to the Philippines)? Staggering sums of money—beyond what any other country or even collection of countries could imagine spending—has poured into the American military and the arms industry that undergirds it and monopolizes the global trade in weaponry. In the process, Washington became a war capital and Barack Obama, as his wife indicated when talking about Trump's victory with Oprah Winfrey, became, above all other presidential functions, the commander-in-chief. ("It is important for the health of this nation," she told Winfrey, "that we support the commander-in-chief.") The president's role in wartime had, of course, always been commander-in-chief, but now that's the position many of us vote for (and that even newspapers endorse), and since war is so permanently embedded in the American way of life now, Donald Trump is guaranteed to remain that for his full term.

And the role has expanded strikingly in these years, as the White House gained the power to make war in just about any fashion it chose without significant reference to Congress. The president now has his own air force of drone assassins to dispatch more or less anywhere on the planet to take out more or less anyone. At the same time, co-cooned inside the military, an elite, secretive second military, the special operations forces, has been expanding its personnel, budget, and operations endlessly, and its most secretive element, the Joint Special Operations Command, might even be thought of as the president's private army.

Meanwhile, the weaponry and advanced technology with which this country has been fighting its never-ending (and remarkably unsuccessful) conflicts abroad—from Predator drones to the StingRay tracking device that mimics a cell tower and so gets nearby phones to connect to it—began migrating home, as America's borders and police forces were militarized. The police have been supplied with weaponry and other equipment directly off the battlefields of Iraq and Afghanistan, while veterans from those wars have joined the proliferation of SWAT teams, the domestic version of special ops teams, that are now a must-have for police departments nationwide.

It's no coincidence that Trump and his generals are eager to pump up a supposedly "depleted" military with yet more funds or, given the history of these years, that he appointed so many retired generals from our losing wars to key "civilian" positions atop that military and the national security state. As with his billionaires, Trump is stamping the real face of twenty-first-century America on Washington.

THE RISE OF THE NATIONAL SECURITY STATE

In these years, a similar process has been underway in relation to the national security state. Vast sums of money have flowed into the country's seventeen intelligence outfits and their secret black budgets, and into the Department of Homeland Security. (Before 9/11, Americans might have associated that word "homeland" with Nazi Germany or the Soviet Union, but never with this country.) New agencies were launched and elaborate headquarters and other complexes built for the expansion of that state-within-a-state, to the tune of billions of dollars. At the same time, it was "privatized," its doors thrown open to the contract employees of a parade of warrior corporations. And, of course, the National Security Agency created a global surveillance apparatus so all-encompassing that it left the fantasies of the totalitarian regimes of the twentieth century in the dust.

As the national security state rose in Washington amid an enveloping shroud of secrecy (and the fierce hounding of whistleblowers), it became the de facto fourth branch of government. Under the circumstances, don't think of it as a happenstance that the 2016 election might have been settled eleven days early thanks to FBI director James Comey's intervention in the race—a historical first for the national security state. However decisive Comey's interference was to the final vote tallies, it certainly caught the mood of the new era that had been birthed in Washington long before Donald Trump's victory. No matter the arguments Trump as president may have with the CIA or other agencies, these institutions will be crucial to his rule (once brought to heel by his appointees).

Those billionaires, generals, and national security chieftains had already been deeply embedded in our American world before Trump made his run for president. They will now be part and parcel of his world going forward.

THE COMING OF THE ONE-PARTY STATE

Thanks to the political developments of these years, and a man with obvious autocratic tendencies entering the Oval Office, it's possible to begin to imagine an American one-party state emerging from the shell of our former democratic system. After all, the Republicans already control the House of Representatives (thanks in significant part to gerrymandering), the Senate, the White House, and assumedly, in the years to come, the Supreme Court. They also control a record thirty-three out of fifty governorships, have tied a record by taking sixty-eight out of the ninety-eight state legislative chambers, and have broken another by gaining control of thirty-three out of fifty full state legislatures. In addition, as the North Carolina legislature has recently shown, the urge among state Republicans to give themselves new, extrademocratic, extralegal powers (as well as a historic Republican drive to restrict the ballot in various ways, claiming defense against nonexistent voter fraud) should be considered a sign of the direction in which we could be headed in a future embattled Trumpist country.

In addition, for years the Democratic Party saw its various traditional bases of support weaken, wither, or, as in the 2016 election, simply opt for a candidate competing for the party's nomination who wasn't even a Democrat. Until this election loss, however, that party was at least a large, functioning political bureaucracy. Today, no one knows quite what it is. It's clear, however, that one of America's two dominant political parties is in a state of disarray and remarkable weakness. Meanwhile, the Republican Party, assumedly the future base for that Trumpian one-party state, is in its own disheveled condition, a party of apparatchiks and ideologues in Washington and embattled factions in the provinces. In many ways, the incipient collapse of the two-party system in a flood of one-percent money cleared the path for Trump's victory.

Unlike the previous three shifts in American life described, however, this one is hardly in place, no less fully institutionalized, and so harder to pin down. Instead, the sense of party chaos and weakness so crucial to the rise of Donald Trump still holds, and the same sense of chaos might be said to apply to the fifth shift.

THE COMING OF THE NEW MEDIA MOMENT

Among the things that prepared the way for Trump, who could leave out the crumbling of the classic newspaper/TV world of news? In these years, it lost much of its traditional advertising base, was bypassed by social media, and the TV part of it found itself in an endless hunt for viewers, normally via 24/7 "news" events, eternally blown out of proportion but easy to cover in a nonstop way by shrinking news staffs. To this end, they searched for anything or anyone (preferably of the celebrity variety) that the public couldn't help staring at, including a

celebrity-turned-politician-turned-provocateur with the world's can-
niest sense of what the media so desperately needed: him. It may have
seemed that Trump inaugurated our new media moment by becoming
the first tweetmeister-in-chief and the shout-out master of that universe, but in truth he merely grasped the nature of our new, chaotic
media moment and ran with it.

A final point: Donald Trump has inherited a land that has been
hollowed out by the new realities that made him a success and allowed
him to sweep to what, to many experts, looked like an improbable
victory. He will preside over a country that is ever less special, a nation
that, as Trump himself has pointed out, has an increasingly shattered
transportation system, an infrastructure that has been drastically de-
based, and an everyday economy that offers fewer jobs or ones of lesser
quality to ever more of his countrymen. It will be an America whose
destructive power only grows but whose ability to translate that into
anything approaching victory eternally recedes.

FIVE

A Quagmire Country

Donald Trump is a messenger from the gods, the deities of empire gone astray. These gods sent us a man without a center, undoubtedly because our country, too, lacks a center, a man without a fixed opinion or a single conviction, except about himself and his family, because this country, too, is now a swirling mess of contradictory beliefs and groups at each other's throats. They sent us our first billionaire president who left countless people holding the bag in his various, often failed, business dealings. He brings to mind that classic phrase "those that sow the wind, shall reap the whirlwind" just as we're now reaping the results of the one-percent politics that gained such traction in recent years, and of a kind of war-making, American style, that initially seemed aimed at global supremacy, but now seems to have no conceivable goal. They sent us a man ready to build a vanity wall on the Mexican border and pour more money into the military at a time when it's becoming harder for Americans to imagine investing in anything but an ever-more powerful national security state, even as the country's infrastructure crumbles. The gods sent us a billionaire who once deep-sixed a startling number of his own businesses to save a country that couldn't be more powerful and yet has proven incapable of building a single mile of high-speed rail. Into this quagmire, the gods dispatched the man who loves the "mother of all bombs," who drools over "my generals," who wants to build a "big, fat, beautiful wall" on our southern border, but was beyond clueless about where power actually lay in Washington.

He's a man with a history but without a sense of history, a man for whom anything is imaginable and everything is mutable, including the past. In this, too, he's symptomatic of the nation he now "leads." Who among us even remembers the set of Washington officials who, only a decade and a half ago, had such glorious dreams about establishing a global *Pax Americana* and who led us so unerringly into an unending hell in the Greater Middle East? Who remembers that those officials of the George W. Bush administration had another dream as well: of a *Pax Republicana,* a one-party imperial state that would stretch across the American South deep into the Midwest, Southwest, and parts of the West, kneecapping the Democratic Party for an eternity and leaving that artifact of a two-party past confined to the country's coastal areas. Their dream—and it couldn't have been more immodest—was to rule the world and its great remaining superpower for . . . well . . . more or less, ever.

The United States would be the land of wealth and power to a previously unimaginable degree. It would be the land that made everything that went bang in the night—and in that (and perhaps that alone) their dreams would be fulfilled. To this day, Hollywood and its action films dominate planetary screens, while American arms merchants have a near monopoly on selling the world their dangerous toys. As our forty-fifth president put it, the energies of the industry and of the American government should remain focused on getting countries across the globe to engage in "the purchase of lots of beautiful military equipment." Indeed.

As for the rest of their dream of geopolitical dominance, it began to come a cropper remarkably quickly. As it turned out, the military that American presidents regularly hailed as the "greatest force for human liberation the world has ever known" or "the finest fighting force in the history of the world" couldn't even win wars against lightly armed insurgents or deal with enemies employing roadside bombs that could be built off the Internet for the price of a pizza. The US military (and its allied warrior corporations) turned out not to be a force for eternal order and triumph but, at least across the Greater Middle East and Africa, for eternal chaos. They were the whirlwind that meant neither the *"pax"* nor the *"Americana"* would come to pass.

While Rome Burned

Meanwhile, back at home, a gerrymandered, near-one-party state did indeed come into existence as the Republicans swept most governorships, gained control of a significant majority of state legislatures, nailed down the House and the Senate, and finally, when Little Big Man entered the Oval Office, took it all. Theirs was a feat for the history books—or so it briefly seemed. Instead, the result has been chaos, thanks in part to a Republican Party that is actually three or four component parties and a president who is barely associated with it, as a war of all against all broke out. None of this should have been surprising, given a congressional party that had in the preceding years honed its skills not on ruling but on blocking rule, and so has largely proved incapable even of ruling itself, no less containing the wild man or his unpredictable team of advisers in the White House.

From his "big, fat, beautiful wall" to his "big league," "phenomenal" tax plan to his "insurance for everybody" healthcare program, the president promises to be the living proof that the long dreamed of *Pax Republicana* is just another form of war without end on the domestic front as well.

Trump's victory was, in a sense, a revelation that both political parties had been hollowed out, as every other Republican presidential candidate was swept unceremoniously off stage and out of contention under a hail of insults. Meanwhile, the Democratic Party, by now a remarkably mindless (and spineless) political machine without much to underpin it, came to seem ever more like the domestic equivalent of those failed states the war on terror was creating in the Greater Middle East. In short, American politics was visibly faltering and, in the whirlwind that deposited Little Big Man in office, an expanding range of Americans seemed in danger of going down, too, including Medicaid users, Obamacare enrollees, meals-on-wheels seniors, and food stamp recipients in what could become a slow-motion collapse of livable lives amid a proliferation of billionaires. Think of us as a nation in the process of consuming itself, even as our president turns the White House into a private business. If this is imperial "decline," it's certainly a curious version of it.

It was into the growing hell that passed for the planet's "sole super-power" that those gods dispatched Little Big Man—not a shape-shifting creature but a man without shape and lacking all fixed ideas (except about himself). He was perfectly capable of saying anything in any situation, and then, in altered circumstances, of saying just the opposite without blinking or evidently even noticing. His May 2017 trip to Saudi Arabia was a classic case of just that. Gone were the election campaign denunciations of the Saudis for their human rights record and for possibly being behind the 9/11 attacks, as well as of Islam as a religion that "hates us"; gone was his criticism of Michelle Obama for not wearing a headscarf on her visit to Riyadh (Melania and Ivanka did the same), and of Barack Obama for bowing to a Saudi king (he did, too). Out the window went his previous insistence that any self-respecting American politician must use the phrase "radical Islamic terrorism," which he carefully avoided. And none of this was different from, say, swearing on the campaign trail that he would never touch Medicaid and then, in his first budget, offering plans to slash $880 billion from that program over the next decade.

Admittedly, Donald Trump has yet to appoint his horse (or perhaps his golf cart) as a senator or, as far as we know, to commit acts of incest, in the tradition of Caligula, the first mad Roman emperor. Yet in many ways, doesn't he feel something like an updated version of Caligula or perhaps of Nero who so famously fiddled—or rather, according to historian Mary Beard in her book *SPQR*, actually played the lyre—while Rome burned?

Fortunately, unlike every psychiatrist in town, I'm not bound by the "Goldwater Rule," which prohibits a diagnosis of a public figure you haven't personally examined. While I have no expertise on whether Donald Trump has a narcissistic personality disorder, I see no reason not to say the obvious: he's a distinctly disturbed individual. That he was nonetheless elected president tells us a good deal about where we are as a country today. As Tony Schwartz, who actually wrote Trump's bestselling book *The Art of the Deal,* put it, "Trump was equally clear with me that he didn't value—nor even necessarily recognize—the qualities that tend to emerge as people grow more secure, such as empathy, generosity, reflectiveness, the capacity to delay gratification or, above all, a conscience, an inner sense of right and wrong."

Now, that should be frightening. After all, given who he is, given his fear of "losing," of rejection, of not being loved (or more accurately, adulated), of, in short, being obliterated, who knows what such a man might do in a crisis, including even obliterating the rest of us. After all, he already lives in a world without fixed boundaries, definitions, or history, which is why nothing he says has real meaning. And yet he himself couldn't be more meaningful. Trump is a message, a warning of the first order, and if that were all he were, he would just be an inadvertent teacher about the nature of our American world and we could indeed thank him and do our best to move on.

Unfortunately, there's another factor to take into account. Humanity had, in the years before his arrival, come up with two quite different and devastating ways of doing ourselves in: one an instant Armageddon, the other a slow-motion trip to hell. Each of them threatens to cripple or destroy the very planet that has nurtured us these tens of thousands of years. It was not, of course, Donald Trump who put us in this peril. He's just a particularly grim reminder of how dangerous our world has truly become.

After all, Little Big Man now has unparalleled access to the most "beautiful" weapons of all and he's eager to update and expand an already vast arsenal of them. I'm talking, of course, about nuclear weapons. Any president we elect has, since the 1950s, had the power to take out the planet. Only once have we come truly close. Nonetheless, for the control over such weaponry to be in the hands of a deeply unpredictable and visibly disturbed president is obviously a danger to us all.

It could be assumed that the gods who sent him into the Oval Office at such a moment have a perverse sense of humor. Certainly, when it comes to the second of those two deadly dangers, climate change, he's already taken action based on another of his fantasies: that making America great again means taking it back to the fossil-fueled 1950s. His ignorance about and actions to increase the effects of climate change have removed the United States, the second-largest emitter of greenhouse gases on the planet, from the climate change sweepstakes and put it in uncharted territory. These acts and the desire to promote fossil fuels in every way imaginable will someday undoubtedly be seen as crimes against humanity. But by then they will already have done their dirty deed.

If luck doesn't hold, Donald Trump may end up making Caligula and Nero look like mere statesmen. If luck doesn't hold, he may be the Littlest Big Man of all.

The Insult Wars in Washington

I don't tweet, but I do have a brief message for our president: Will you please get the hell out of the way for a few minutes? You and your antics are blocking our view of the damn world and it's a world we should be focusing on!

Maybe it was the moment when I found myself reading Donald Trump's two-part tweet aimed at MSNBC's Joe Scarborough and Mika Brzezinski who, on their show *Morning Joe*, had suggested that the president was "possibly unfit mentally."

"I heard," the president tweeted, "poorly rated @Morning_Joe speaks badly of me (don't watch anymore). Then how come low I.Q. Crazy Mika, along with Psycho Joe, came . . . to Mar-a-Lago 3 nights in a row around New Year's Eve, and insisted on joining me. She was bleeding badly from a face-lift. I said no!"

In response to Trump's eerie fascination with women's blood, Brzezinski tweeted a shot of the back of a Cheerios box that had the phrase "Made for Little Hands" on it. And so it all began, days of it, including the anti-cyberbullying First Lady's rush (however indirectly) to her husband's side via her communications director who said, "As the First Lady has stated publicly in the past, when her husband gets attacked, he will punch back 10 times harder."

But one tweet truly caught my attention, even if it was at the very beginning of a donnybrook that, with twists, turns, and Trumpian rejoinders of every sort, would monopolize the headlines and fill the yak-o-sphere of cable TV for days. That tweet came from conservative idol Bill Kristol, editor at large for the *Weekly Standard*. It said: "Dear @realDonaldTrump, You are a pig. Sincerely, Bill Kristol."

Strange, but at that moment another moment—so distant it might as well have been from a different planet or, as indeed was the case, another century—came to my mind. Donald Trump was still finishing his high school years at a military academy and I was a freshman at Yale. It would have been a weekend in the late spring of 1963. One of my roommates was a working-class kid from Detroit, more of a rarity at that elite all-male school than this New York Jew (in the years when Yale had just removed its Jewish quotas). And here was another rarity: we had a double date with two young women from a local New Haven Catholic college.

That night, out of pure ignorance, we violated Yale's parietal hours—a reality from another century that no one even knows about anymore. Those young women stayed in our rooms beyond the time the school considered . . . well, in that world of WASPs, "kosher" might not be the perfect word, but you get what I mean. Let me hasten to add that, in those forbidden minutes, I don't believe I even exchanged a kiss with my date.

(Note to readers: Be patient. Think of this as my version of a shaggy dog—or perhaps an over-combed Donald—tale. But rest assured that I haven't forgotten our tweeter-in-chief, not for a second. How could I?)

Anyway, the four of us left our room just as a campus cop was letting another student, who had locked himself out, back into the room opposite ours. When he saw us, he promptly demanded our names and recorded them in his notebook for violating parietal hours (which meant we were in genuine trouble). As he walked down the stairs, my roommate, probably a little drunk, leaned over the banister and began shouting at him. More than half a century later, I have no memory of what exactly he yelled—with the exception of a single word. As Bill Kristol did the other day with our president, he called that cop a "pig."

Now, I wasn't a working-class kid. In the worst of times for my parents, the "golden" 1950s when my father was in debt and often out of work, I was already being groomed to move up the American class ladder. I was in spirit upper middle class in the fashion of that moment. I was polite to a T and a genuine good boy of that era. And good boys didn't imagine that, in real life, even with a couple of beers under your belt, anyone would ever call the campus version of a policeman, a "pig." I had never in my life heard such a thing. It simply wasn't the way you talked to the police then, or (until last week) the way you spoke to or of American presidents. Not even Donald Trump.

In other words, when Kristol of all people did that, it shocked me. Which means, to my everlasting shame, that I must still be a good boy, even if now of a distinctly antediluvian sort. Mind you, within years of that incident, it had become a commonplace for activists of the left (though, I must admit, never me) to call the police—the ones out in the streets hassling antiwar protesters, black activists, and others—"pigs." Or rather, "the pigs."

So here's a question I'm now asking myself: If Kristol can do it with impunity, then why not Tom Engelhardt, fifty-four years later? Why not me, all these years after American presidents began ordering death and mayhem without surcease; green-lighting secret prisons and torture; invading and occupying countries around the world; sending robotic assassins across the planet to execute, on their say-so alone, those they identified as terrorists or enemies (and anyone else in the vicinity, children included); helping uproot populations in numbers not seen since World War II; overseeing the creation of a global and domestic surveillance state the likes of which would have stunned the totalitarian rulers of the twentieth century; and pumping more money into the US military budget than that spent by the next eight major states combined, which of course is just to start down a long list?

Under the circumstances, why not bring a barnyard animal to bear on the twenty-first-century American presidency, the office that in its glory days decades ago used to be referred to as "the imperial presidency"? After all, Donald Trump is no anomaly in the Oval Office, even when, as with Scarborough and Brzezinski, he tweets and rants in a startlingly anomalous fashion for a president. He is instead a bizarre symptom of American decline, of the very thing he staked his presidential run on: the fact that this country is no longer "great."

Of course, tactically, engaging in name-calling with Donald Trump is essentially aiding and abetting his presidency (something the media does daily, even hourly). He and his advisers are of a schoolyard sticks-and-stones-will-break-my-bones-but-names-will-never-hurt-me mentality. As the *Washington Post* reported, they consider such insult wars a form of "winning" and a way to eternally engage the "fake news media" on grounds they consider advantageous, in a way that will endlessly stoke the president's still loyal base.

To my mind, however, that's hardly the most essential problem with such language. I suspect that the tweets and insults—whether Trump's, Scarborough's, or Kristol's—act as a kind of smoke screen. In readership and viewership terms, they're manna from heaven for the very "fake news media" Trump loves to hate. In the process, however, the blood, the pigs, and all the rest of the package of Washington's insult wars keep our eyes endlessly glued on the president and on next to nothing else in our world. They blind us to our planet and its troubles.

Can there be any question that Donald Trump's greatest talent is his eternal ability to suck the air out of the media room? It was a skill he demonstrated in stunning fashion during the 2016 election campaign, accumulating an unprecedented $5 billion or so in free media coverage on his way to the White House. Trump looms larger than life, larger than anything in our screen-rich world. He essentially blocks the view, day and night.

In that sense—in the closest I've probably come to such an insult myself—I've labeled him our own Little Big Man. He's petty, small in so many ways, but he looms so large, tweet by bloody tweet, that it's hard to see the burning forest for the one flaming tree.

The Overheated Present and an Overheating Future

On June 30, 2017, when the Scarborough–Brzezinski brouhaha was going full blast, Trump met with the new South Korean president, Moon Jae-in, and the two of them spoke to the media in the White House Rose Garden, taking no questions. The president's comments on the Korean situation were strikingly grim and blunt. "The era of strategic patience with the North Korean regime," he said, "has failed.

Frankly, that patience is over." He then added, "We have many options with respect to North Korea."

As it happens, we know a little about the nature of those "options." Only the day before, Trump's national security advisor, Lieutenant General H. R. McMaster, confirmed reports that a new set of options had indeed been prepared for the president. "What we have to do," he told a Washington think tank, "is prepare all options because the president has made clear to us that he will not accept a nuclear power in North Korea and a threat that can target the United States and target the American population." As McMaster himself made clear, "all options" included new military ones.

Leaving its still modest but threatening nuclear arsenal aside, the conventional firepower the North Koreans have arrayed along their border with South Korea and aimed at Seoul, a city of twenty-five million only thirty miles away, is believed to be potentially devastating. Add to that the 28,500 US troops stationed in the country, most relatively close to that border, not to speak of the 200,000 American civilians living there, and you undoubtedly have one of the most explosive spots on the planet. If hostilities broke out and spiraled out of control, as they might, countless people could die, nuclear weapons could indeed be used for the first time since 1945, and parts of Asia could be ravaged (including, possibly, areas of Japan). What a second Korean War might mean, in other words, is almost beyond imagining.

At the Trump–Moon Rose Garden event, the president also announced both sanctions against a Chinese bank linked to North Korea and a $1.4 billion arms sale to Taiwan, clearly meant as slaps at the Chinese leadership. In other words, when it came to getting China's help on the Korean situation, Trump's "strategic patience," which bloomed in early April at a Mar-a-Lago meeting with Chinese president Xi Jinping, seemed to have worn out in mere months.

In this context, if you thought that the Trump-Scarborough-Brzezinski feud was a tinderbox, think again. Did we hear anything about the Korean news? On that Saturday morning, the *New York Times* made "The Battle of 'Morning Joe': A Presidential Feud" its front-page focal piece (with a carryover full page of coverage inside, including a second piece on the subject and that day's lead editorial, "Mr.

Trump, Melting Under Criticism"). As for the Korean story, it made the bottom of page eight ("Trump Adopts a More Aggressive Stance with US Allies and Adversaries in Asia") and didn't even mention the president's "strategic patience" comments until its sixteenth paragraph. There was also a page eight story on Trump's Chinese bank sanctions and arms deal with Taiwan.

And in this the *Times* was anything but atypical. Under the circumstances, you might be forgiven for thinking that the greatest story in our world (and its greatest danger) now lies in the tweet-o-sphere. It took the first North Korean test of an intercontinental ballistic missile, carefully scheduled for July 4th, to break that country into the news in a noticeable way and even then, Trump's tweets were at the center of the reportage.

Similarly, if Trump and his antics didn't take up so much room in our present American world, it might be easier to take in so many other potential dangers on a planet where matches seem in good supply and the kindling prepared for burning. You could look to the Middle East, for example, and the quickly morphing war against ISIS, which could soon become a Trump administration–lit fire involving Turkey, Iran, Saudi Arabia, Qatar, and even Russia, among other states and groups. Or you could look to the possible future passage of some version of a Republican health care bill and the more than 200,000 preventable deaths that would be likely to result from it in the coming decade.

Or you could focus on a president who has turned his back on the Paris Agreement and is now plugging not just North American "energy independence" but full-scale "American energy dominance" on a planet on which he promises a new fossil-fueled "golden age for America." In such an age, with such a president—if you'll excuse the word—hogging the limelight, who's even thinking about the estimated 1.4 billion "climate change refugees" who could be produced by 2060 as the world's lowlands flood? For comparison, according to the UN Refugee Agency the 2016 figure on "forcibly displaced people" globally, which set a post–World War II record, is 65.6 million, a staggering number that would be but a drop in the bucket in our overheating future if those 2060 estimates prove even close to accurate.

A World of a Tweeter-in-Chief and "Some Stirred-Up Moslems"

Donald Trump's recent tweets do make one thing clear: we've been on quite an American journey over the last four decades, one that could be thought of as a voyage from Brzezinski (Jimmy Carter's national security advisor, Zbigniew, who died in May 2017) to Brzezinski (Mika, his daughter).

In a way, you might say that, back in 1979, Brzezinski, the father, first ushered us into a new global age of imperial conflict. He was, after all, significantly responsible for ensuring that the United States would engage in a war in Afghanistan in order to give the Soviet Union its own Vietnam. He launched what would become a giant CIA-organized, Saudi- and Pakistani-backed program for funding, training, and arming the most fundamental of Afghan fundamentalists, and other anti-Soviet jihadists, including a young Saudi by the name of Osama bin Laden. (President Ronald Reagan would later term those Afghan Islamist rebels "the moral equal of our Founding Fathers.") In doing so, Brzezinski set in motion a process that would drive an Islamic wedge deep into the heart of the Soviet Union and, after Soviet intervention in Afghanistan resulted in a disastrous decade-long war, send the Red Army limping home in defeat, all of which would, in turn, play a role in the implosion of the Soviet Union.

On this subject, Brzezinski would be forever unrepentant. As he said in 1998, "What is most important to the history of the world? The Taliban or the collapse of the Soviet empire? Some stirred-up Moslems or the liberation of Central Europe and the end of the Cold War?" And as for those millions of Afghans who would end up dead, wounded, or uprooted from their homes and lives as a result, well, really, who cared?

We are now fully in that world of "stirred-up Moslems" and, as it happens, the United States is still fighting a war in Afghanistan as the Trump administration gets ready to surge militarily there, for perhaps the fourth or fifth time since October 2001. And who's even paying attention? Who could with the latest presidential tweets headlining the news and all-hands-on-deck in Washington for the insult wars?

Who woulda thunk that between 1979 and 2017 the United States would twice find itself at war (for more than a cumulative quarter century so far) in, of all places, Afghanistan, with a billionaire president, literally a casino capitalist, now running the White House as an adjunct to his family business and sending out bizarre messages about Zbigniew Brzezinski's daughter Mika, to a media obsessed with covering that as the news of the moment?

Make America great again? You must be kidding. It's time to stop insulting pigs and focus instead on the state of our planet.

Who? Us?

I find it strange that no one who matters here seems to feel the slightest responsibility for the planet's dismal state. All the politicians, power players, and pundits in Washington who wouldn't have hesitated to take complete credit, had the United States achieved anything like its fantasy of a *Pax Americana* world, couldn't be quicker these days to place the responsibility for what's actually happened elsewhere.

The Russian president now gets much of the blame in Washington for the sorry mess of our world, from Eastern Europe and the unsettled NATO alliance to Syria. As for where the rest of the blame lands, it's the Chinese, of course, who have had the nerve to flex their potential great-power muscles by bulking up their military, building fake "islands" in the South China Sea, and claiming parts of that body of water as their own, while not pressuring the North Koreans harder to stand down. It's the Iranians who somehow are responsible for much of the mess in the Middle East, along with various jihadi successors to and spin-offs from the original al-Qaeda. They take the rest of the blame for the world of chaos that continues to spread across the Greater Middle East, parts of Africa, and now the Philippines—not to mention the refugees fleeing those embattled and desperate lands who are, we are regularly assured, threatening the continental United States with disastrous harm.

I don't mean to say that such a crew (refugees excepted) shouldn't bear some of the blame for our disintegrating world, but just remind me: Wasn't the Islamic State born in an American military prison in

Iraq? Weren't the Iranian theocrats, those Great Satan haters, born in the grim crucible of the shah's rule (and that of his brutal secret police) after the CIA helped hatch a coup that overthrew the elected prime minister of that country in 1953? Didn't Washington ignore promises made to former Soviet leader Mikhail Gorbachev and others and instead do its damnedest to move NATO's line of control into parts of the former Soviet empire and associated satellite states?

Didn't the Bush administration lump North Korea in with Iraq, a nation it was eager to invade, and Iran, another country it planned to take down sooner or later, as the infamous "axis of evil," even though the North Koreans had nothing to do with either of those countries? In the most public manner possible, in a State of the Union address to the nation, President George W. Bush associated all three of those countries with terrorism and evil in what was unmistakably a "regime change" package. If you were eager to convince the North Korean leadership that possessing a nuclear arsenal was the only way to go, that certainly was a good start. And didn't President Bush and his officials functionally shred the Clinton-negotiated agreement by which the North Koreans had indeed frozen their nuclear program, in part by listing the country in their 2002 *Nuclear Posture Review* "as one of the states that might become the target of a preventive strike"?

And which country was it that only recently announced its withdrawal from the Paris climate agreement, the crucial global architecture for protecting the planetary environment, and so humanity's future, from a grim kind of dismemberment?

Don't we Americans have any responsibility for the situation we now face globally, from North Korea to the Greater Middle East, Ukraine to Venezuela? Didn't the actions of America's leaders and its national security state have anything to do with the world that called forth the Trumpian wave, which could now swamp so many ships of state? Maybe President Trump can indeed pardon himself (an issue being debated by constitutional scholars), but who has pardoned everyone else who lent a hand, large or small, to the creation of what increasingly looks like a failed world?

Are there no high crimes and misdemeanors for which we Americans are responsible on a planet of the otherwise guilty?

In truth, in every land across the Greater Middle East and Africa where the US military has gotten involved in hostilities, from Libya to Iraq, Yemen to Afghanistan, it has left shaken or failed states and spreading terror movements. It has been a major player in a decade and a half of disaster that has helped destabilize significant parts of the planet. And yet when it comes to apportioning blame, the main people tarred with the disaster that's been the war on terror are the untold numbers who have been made into refugees in its wake, those who, we are told, would be a mortal danger to us, were we to welcome them to our country.

In such a global context, our Congress has been eager indeed to sanction the Russians, the Iranians, and the North Koreans for their roles in spreading misery, but who's going to sanction us? Honestly, don't you wonder how we got off the hook so easily for the world we swore that we alone would create? Isn't the United States responsible for anything? Doesn't anyone even remember?

We now have a president with the strangest demeanor, a narcissistic bully spouting a rhetoric that eerily echoes the bellicose threats of North Korea. However, like the spreading terror movements and failed states of the Greater Middle East, he, too, should be seen as a spawn of the actions, programs, and dreams of the world's sole superpower in its self-proclaimed years of glory and of its plans for a military-enforced global *Pax Americana*. By the time he's done, President Trump may be responsible for high crimes, including nuclear ones, of a sort that even impeachment wouldn't cover.

Blame the evildoers for the devastation visiting this planet? Sure thing. But the United States? Not for a second.

Welcome to the post-American world.

SIX

The Honeymoon of the Generals

Donald Trump, whatever else he may be, is distinctly a creature of history. He's unimaginable without it. This, in turn, means that the radical nature of his presidency should serve as a reminder of just how radically the fifteen years after 9/11 reshaped American life, politics, and governance. In that sense, to generalize (excuse the pun), Trump's early days in the Oval Office already offer a strikingly vivid and accurate portrait of the America we've been living in for some years now, even if we'd prefer to pretend otherwise.

After all, his is clearly a government of, by, and evidently for the billionaires and the generals, which pretty much sums up where we've been heading anyway. Let's start with those generals. In the fifteen years before Trump entered the Oval Office, Washington became a permanent war capital; war, a permanent feature of our American world; and the military, the most admired institution in American life, the one in which we, the people, have the most confidence among an otherwise fading crew, including the presidency, the Supreme Court, public schools, banks, television news, newspapers, big business, and Congress (in descending order).

Support for that military in the form of staggering sums of tax-payer dollars is one of the few things congressional Democrats and

Republicans can still agree on. The military-industrial complex rides ever higher; police across the country have been armed like military forces, while the technology of war from America's distant battlefields —from StingRays to MRAPs to military surveillance drones—has come home big time, and we've been SWATified.

This country has been militarized in all sorts of ways, both obvious and less so, in a fashion that Americans once might not have imagined possible. Declaring and making war has increasingly become—the Constitution be damned—the sole prerogative of the White House without significant reference to Congress. Meanwhile, thanks to the drone assassination program run directly out of the Oval Office, the president has become an assassin-in-chief as well as commander-in-chief.

Under the circumstances, no one should have been surprised when Donald Trump turned to the very generals he criticized in the election campaign, men who fought fifteen years of losing wars they bitterly feel should have been won. In his government, they have now taken over—a historic first—what had largely been the civilian posts of secretary of defense, secretary of Homeland Security, national security advisor, and National Security Council chief of staff. It should be considered a junta light, and little more than the next logical step in the further militarization of this country.

It's striking, for instance, that when the president finally fired his national security advisor, Michael Flynn, twenty-four days into his presidency, all but one of the other figures that he reportedly considered for a post often occupied by a civilian were retired generals (and an admiral)—or, in the case of the person he actually tapped to be his second national security advisor, H. R. McMaster, a still-active Army general. This reflects a distinct American reality of the twenty-first century that The Donald has simply absorbed like the human sponge he is. As a result, America's permanent wars, each a relative disaster of one sort or another, will now be overseen by men who were, for the last decade and a half, deeply implicated in them. It's a formula for further disaster, but no matter.

Other future Trumpian steps—like the possible mobilization of the National Guard, more than half a century after guardsmen helped desegregate the University of Alabama, to carry out the mass deportation of illegal immigrants—will undoubtedly be in the same mold. In short, we now live in an America of the generals and that would be the case even if Donald Trump had never been elected president.

Add in one more factor of our moment: we have the first signs that members of the military high command may no longer feel bound by the classic American prohibition on taking any part in politics. General Raymond "Tony" Thomas, head of the elite US Special Operations Command, speaking at a conference, essentially warned the president that we as a country are "at war" and that chaos in the White House is not good for the warriors. That's as close as we've come in our time to direct public military criticism of the White House.

The Ascendancy of the Billionaires

As for those billionaires, let's start this way: a billionaire is now president of the United States, something that, until this country was transformed into a one-percent society with one-percent politics, would have been inconceivable. (The closest we came in modern times was Nelson Rockefeller as vice president, and he was appointed by President Gerald Ford in 1974, not elected.) In addition, never have there been so many billionaires and multimillionaires in a cabinet—and that, in turn, was only possible because there are now so staggeringly many billionaires and multimillionaires in this country to choose from. In 1987, there were 41 billionaires in the United States; in 2015, there were 536. What else should be said about the intervening years, which featured growing inequality and the worst economic meltdown since 1929 that only helped strengthen the new version of the American system?

In swift order we moved from billionaires funding the political system to billionaires actually heading and running the government. As a result, we can count on a country even friendlier to the already fantastically wealthy—thanks in part to whatever Trump-style "tax cuts" are put in place—and so the possible establishment of a new "era of dynastic wealth." From the crew of rich dismantlers and destroyers Donald Trump has appointed to his cabinet, expect, among other things, that the privatization of the government—a process until now largely focused on melding warrior corporations with various parts of the national security state—will proceed apace in the rest of the governing apparatus.

We were already living in a different America before November 8, 2016. Donald Trump has merely shoved that reality directly in all our faces. And, indeed, if it weren't for the one-percentification of the United States and the surge of automation (as well as globalization) that destroyed so many jobs and only helped inequality flourish, white working-class Americans, in particular, would not have felt so left behind in the heartland of their own country and so ready to send such an explosive figure into the White House as a visible form of *screw-you*-style protest.

Finally, one other hallmark of the first month of the Trump presidency: the "feud" between the new president and the intelligence sector of the national security state. In these post–9/11 years, that state-within-a-state—sometimes referred to by its critics as the "deep state," though given the secrecy that envelops it, "dark state" might be a more accurate term—grew by leaps and bounds. In that period, for instance, the United States gained a second Defense Department in the form of the Department of Homeland Security, surrounded by its own security-industrial complex, while the intelligence agencies expanded in just about every way imaginable. In those years, they gained a previously inconceivable kind of clout, as well as the ability to essentially listen in on and monitor the communications of just about anyone on the planet (including Americans). Fed copiously by taxpayer dollars, swollen by hundreds of thousands of private contractors from warrior corporations, largely free of the controlling hand of either Congress or the courts, and operating under the kind of blanket secrecy that left most Americans in the dark about its activities (except when whistleblowers revealed its workings), the national security state gained ascendancy in Washington as the de facto fourth branch of government.

Now, key people within its shadowy precincts find Donald Trump, the president who is in so many ways a product of the same processes that elevated them, not to their liking—even less so once he compared their activities to those of the Nazi era. In response, they seem to have gone to war with him and his administration via a remarkable stream of leaks of damaging information, especially about now-departed national security advisor Michael Flynn. As Amanda Taub and Max Fisher of the *New York Times* wrote, "For concerned government officials, leaks may have become one of the few remaining means by which to influence not just Mr. Flynn's policy initiatives but the threat he seemed to pose to their place in democracy."

This represented a version of whistleblowing that, when directed at them in the pre-Trump era, they found appalling. That flood of leaks, while discomfiting Donald Trump, also represented a potential challenge to the American political system as it was once known. When the fiercest defenders of that system begin to be seen as coming from inside the intelligence community and the military, you know that you're in a different and far more perilous world.

Although so much of what's now happening may seem startlingly new and overwhelming, in truth, it's been in development for years, even if the specifics of the Trump presidency were recently unimaginable. We're now living in Donald Trump's America. We're living, that is, in an ever-more chaotic and aberrant land run (to the extent it's run at all) by billionaires and retired generals, and overseen by a distinctly aberrant president at war with aberrant parts of the national security state. That, in a nutshell, is the America created in the post–9/11 years. While this country may have failed dismally in its efforts to invade, occupy, and remake Iraq in its own image, it seems to have invaded, occupied, and remade itself with remarkable success. And we can't blame this one on the Russians.

No one said it better than French king Louis XV: *Après moi, le Trump.*

Institutionalizing War and Its Generals

"MOAB" sounds more like an incestuous, war-torn biblical kingdom than the GBU-43/B Massive Ordnance Air Blast, aka the "mother of all bombs." Still, Donald Trump deserves credit. Only the really, really big bombs, whether North Korean nukes or those 21,600 pounds of MOAB, truly get his attention. Although he wasn't even involved in the decision to drop the largest non-nuclear bomb in the US arsenal for the first time in war, his beloved generals—"We have the best military people on Earth"—already know the man they work for, and the bigger, flashier, more explosive, and winninger, the better.

It was undoubtedly the awesome look of that first MOAB going off in grainy black and white on Fox News, rather than in Afghanistan, that appealed to the president. Just as he was visibly thrilled by all those picturesque Tomahawk cruise missiles, the equivalent of nearly three MOABs, whooshing from the decks of destroyers in the eastern Mediterranean and heading, like so many fabulous fireworks, toward a Syrian airfield. "We've just fired fifty-nine missiles," he said, "all of which hit, by the way, unbelievable, from, you know, hundreds of miles away, all of which hit, amazing. . . . It's so incredible. It's brilliant. It's genius. Our technology, our equipment, is better than anybody by a factor of five."

Call it thrilling. Call it a blast. Call it escalation. Or just call it the age of Trump. ("If you look at what's happened over the last eight weeks and compare that really to what's happened over the past eight years, you'll see there's a tremendous difference, tremendous difference," he commented, adding about MOAB, "This was another very, very successful mission.")

Anyway, here we are and, as so many of his critics have pointed out, the plaudits have been pouring in from all the usual media and political suspects for a president with big enough . . . well, hands, to impressively make war. In our world, this is what now passes for "presidential."

These days, from Syria to Afghanistan, the Koreas to Somalia, Yemen to Iraq, it's easy enough to see Commander-in-Chief Donald Trump as something new under the sun. (It has a different ring to it when the commander-in-chief says, "You're fired!") That missile strike in Syria was a first (Obama didn't dare); the MOAB in Afghanistan was a breakthrough; the drone strikes in Yemen soon after he took office were an absolute record! As for those regular Army troops heading for Somalia, that hasn't happened in twenty-four years! Civilian casualties in the region: rising impressively!

This is mission creep on steroids. At the very least, it seems like evidence that the man who, as a presidential candidate, swore he'd "bomb the shit" out of ISIS and let the US military win again is doing just that. (As he also said on the campaign trail with appropriately placed air punches, "You gotta knock the hell out of them! Boom! Boom! Boom!")

He's lifted restraints on how his commanders in the field can act (hence those soaring civilian casualty figures), let them send more military personnel into Iraq, Syria, and the region generally, taken the constraints off the CIA's drone assassination campaigns, and dispatched an aircraft carrier strike group somewhat indirectly to the waters off the Koreas (with a strike force of tweets and threats accompanying it).

And there's obviously more to come: potentially more troops for Syria; a possible mini-surge of them into Afghanistan (that MOAB strike might have been a canny signal from an American commander "seeking to showcase Afghanistan's myriad threats" to a president who had been paying no attention); a heightened air campaign in Somalia; and that's just to start what will surely be a far longer list in a presidency in which, whether or not infrastructure is ever successfully rebuilt in America, the infrastructure of the military-industrial complex will only continue to grow.

The Chameleon Presidency

President Trump did one thing decisively. He empowered a set of generals or retired generals—James "Mad Dog" Mattis as secretary of defense, H. R. McMaster as national security advisor, and John Kelly as secretary of Homeland Security—men already deeply implicated in America's failing wars across the Greater Middle East. Not being a details guy himself, he's left them to do their damnedest. "What I do is I authorize my military," he told reporters in April 2017. "We have given them total authorization and that's what they're doing and, frankly, that's why they've been so successful lately."

At the hundred-day mark of his presidency, there was no serious reassessment of America's endless wars or how to fight them, no less end them. Instead, there was a recommitment to doing more of the familiar, more of what hasn't worked over the last decade and a half. No one should be surprised by this, given the cast of characters—men who held command posts in those unsuccessful wars and are clearly incapable of thinking about them in other terms than the ones that have been indelibly engrained in the brains of the military high command since soon after 9/11.

That new ruling reality of our American world should offer a hint about the nature of Donald Trump's presidency. It should be a reminder that as strange—okay, bizarre—as his statements, tweets, and acts may have been, as chaotic as his all-in-the-family administration is proving to be, as little as he may resemble anyone we've ever seen in the White House before, he's a logical endpoint to a grim process, whether you're talking about the growth of inequality and the rise of plutocracy or the form that American war-making is taking under him.

When it comes to war and the military, none of what's happened would have been conceivable without the two previous presidencies. None of it would have been possible without Congress's willingness to pump endless piles of money into the Pentagon and the military-industrial complex in the post–9/11 years, without the build-up of the national security state and its various major intelligence outfits, or without the institutionalization of war as a permanent (yet strangely distant) feature of American life and of wars across the Greater Middle East and parts of Africa that evidently can't be won or lost but only carried on into eternity. None of this would have been possible without the growing militarization of this country, without a media rife with retired generals and other former commanders narrating and commenting on the acts of their successors and protégés, and without a political class of Washington pundits and politicians taught to revere that military.

However original Donald Trump may look, he's the curious culmination of old news and a changing country. Given his bravado and braggadocio, it's easy to forget the kinds of militarized extremity that preceded him.

After all, it wasn't Donald Trump who had the hubris, in the wake of 9/11, to declare a "Global War on Terror" against sixty countries (the "swamp" to be drained of that moment). It wasn't Donald Trump who manufactured false intelligence on the weapons of mass destruction Iraq's Saddam Hussein supposedly possessed or who produced bogus claims about that autocrat's connections to al-Qaeda, and then used both to lead the United States into a war on and occupation of his country. It wasn't Donald Trump who invaded Iraq (regardless of whether he was for or against the invasion at the time). It wasn't Donald Trump who donned a flight suit and landed on an aircraft carrier off the coast of San Diego to personally declare that hostilities there were at an end just as they were truly beginning, and to do so under an inane "Mission Accomplished" banner prepared by the White House.

It wasn't Donald Trump who ordered the CIA to kidnap terror suspects (including totally innocent individuals) off the streets of global cities as well as from the backlands of the planet and transport them to foreign prisons or CIA "black sites" where they could be tortured. It wasn't Donald Trump who caused one terror suspect to experience the sensation of drowning eighty-three times in a single month (even if he was inspired by such reports to claim that he would bring torture back as president).

It wasn't Donald Trump who spent eight years in the Oval Office presiding over a global "kill list," running "Terror Tuesday" meetings, and personally helping choose individuals around the world for the CIA to assassinate using what, in essence, was the president's own private drone force, while being praised (or criticized) for his "caution."

It wasn't Donald Trump who presided over the creation of a secret military of seventy thousand elite troops cosseted inside the larger military, special ops personnel who, in recent years, have been dispatched on missions to a large majority of the countries on the planet without the knowledge, no less the consent, of the American people. Nor was it Donald Trump who managed to raise the Pentagon budget to $600 billion and the overall national security budget to something like a trillion dollars or more, even as America's civilian infrastructure aged and buckled. It wasn't Donald Trump who lost an estimated $60 billion to fraud and waste in the "reconstruction" of Iraq and Afghanistan, or who decided to build highways to nowhere and a gas station in the middle of nowhere in Afghanistan.

It wasn't Donald Trump who sent in the warrior corporations to squander more in that single country than was spent on the post–World War II Marshall Plan to put all of Western Europe back on its feet. Nor did he instruct the US military to dump at least $25 billion into rebuilding, retraining, and rearming an Iraqi army that would collapse in 2014 in the face of a relatively small number of ISIS militants, or at least $65 billion into an Afghan army that would turn out to be filled with ghost soldiers.

In its history, the United States has engaged in quite a remarkable range of wars and conflicts. Nonetheless, in the last fifteen years, forever war has been institutionalized as a feature of everyday life in Washington. When Donald Trump won the presidency and inherited those wars and that capital, there was, in a sense, no one left in the remarkably bankrupt political universe of Washington but those generals.

As the chameleon he is, Trump promptly adopted the coloration of the militarized world he had entered and appointed "his" three generals to key security posts. If such a decision seemed anomalous and out of the American tradition, that was only because, unlike Donald Trump, most of the rest of us hadn't caught up with where that "tradition" had actually taken us.

The previous two presidents had played the warrior regularly, donning military outfits—in his presidential years, George W. Bush often looked like a G.I. Joe doll—and saluting troops, while praising them to the skies, as the American people were in their turn trained to do. In the Trump era, however, it's the warriors who are playing the president.

Think of Trump as a chameleon among presidents and much of this makes more sense. A Republican who had been a Democrat for significant periods of his life, he conceivably could have run as a more nativist version of Bernie Sanders on the Democratic ticket, had the political cards been dealt just a little differently. He's a man who has changed himself repeatedly to fit his circumstances and he's doing so again in the Oval Office.

In the world of the media, it's stylish to be shocked, shocked that the president who campaigned on one set of issues and came into office still championing them is now supporting quite a different set—from

China to taxes, NATO to the Export-Import Bank. But this isn't faintly strange: Donald Trump isn't either a politician or a trendsetter; if anything, he's a trend-senser. (In a similar fashion, he didn't create reality TV, nor was he at its origins. He simply perfected a form that was already in development.)

If you want to know just where we are in an America that has been on the march toward a different sort of society and governing system for a long time now, look at him. He's the originator of nothing, but he tells you all you need to know. On war, too, we should think of Trump as a chameleon. War is working for him domestically, whatever it may be doing in the actual world, so he loves it. For the moment, those generals are indeed "his" and their wars his to embrace.

Normally, on entering the Oval Office, presidents receive what the media calls a "honeymoon" period. Things go well. Praise is forthcoming. Approval ratings are heart-warming. Donald Trump got none of this. His approval ratings quickly headed for the honeymoon cellar or maybe the honeymoon fallout shelter; the media and he went to war; and one attempt after another to fulfill his promises—from executive orders on deportation to repealing Obamacare and building his wall—have come a cropper. His administration seems to be in eternal chaos, the cast of characters changing by the week or tweet, and few key secondary posts being filled.

In only one area has Donald Trump experienced that promised honeymoon: think of it as the honeymoon of the generals. He gave them "total authorization," and the missiles left the ships, the drones flew, and the giant bomb dropped. Even when the results were disappointing, if not disastrous (as in a raid on Yemen in which a US special operator was killed, children slaughtered, and nothing of value recovered), he still somehow stumbled into highly praised "presidential" moments.

So far, the generals are the only ones who have delivered for him, big league. As a result, he's given them even more authority to do whatever they want, while hugging them tighter yet. Here's the problem, though: there's a predictable element to all of this and it doesn't work in Donald Trump's favor. America's forever wars have been pursued by these generals and others like them for more than fifteen years and there's no reason to believe that further military action will, a decade and a half later, produce more positive results.

What happens, then? What happens when the war honeymoon is over and the generals keep right on fighting the war on terror their way? The last two presidents put up with permanent failing war, making the best they could of it. That's unlikely for Donald Trump. When the praise begins to die down, the criticism starts to rise, and questions are asked, watch out.

What then? In a world of plutocrats and generals, what coloration will Donald Trump take on next? Who will be left, except Jared and Ivanka?

The Winningest President and the Losingest Generals

The most surprising winner of our era and possibly—to put ourselves fully in the Trumpian spirit—of any era since the first protozoan stalked the Earth entered the Oval Office on January 20, 2017, and promptly surrounded himself with a set of generals from America's failed wars of the post–9/11 era. In other words, the man who repeatedly promised that in his presidency Americans would win to the point of tedium—"We're going to win so much, you're going to be so sick and tired of winning, you're going to come to me and go 'Please, please, we can't win anymore'"—promptly chose to elevate the losingest guys in town. If reports are to be believed, he evidently did this because of his military school background, his longstanding crush on General George Patton of World War II fame (or at least the movie version of him), and despite having actively avoided military service himself in the Vietnam years, his weak spot for four stars with tough monikers like "Mad Dog."

During the election campaign, Trump himself was surprisingly clear-eyed when it came to the nature of American generalship in the twenty-first century. As he put it, "Under the leadership of Barack Obama and Hillary Clinton, the generals have been reduced to rubble, reduced to a point where it is embarrassing for our country." On coming to power, however, Trump reached into that rubble to choose his guys. In the years before he ran, he had been no less clear-eyed on the war he as president extended in Afghanistan. Of that conflict, he typically tweeted in 2013, "We have wasted an enormous amount of blood and treasure in Afghanistan. Their government has zero appreciation. Let's get out!"

The careers of his three chosen generals are inextricably linked to America's losing wars. Then-Colonel H. R. McMaster gained his reputation in 2005 by leading the 3rd Armored Cavalry Regiment into the Iraqi city of Tal Afar and "liberating" it from Sunni insurgents, while essentially introducing the counterinsurgency tactics that would become the heart and soul of General David Petraeus's 2007 "surge" in Iraq.

Only one small problem: McMaster's much-publicized "victory," like so many other American military successes of this era, didn't last. A year later, Tal Afar was "awash in sectarian violence," wrote Jon Finer, a *Washington Post* reporter who accompanied McMaster into that city. It would be among the first Iraqi cities taken by Islamic State militants in 2014 and was not "liberated" (again) until 2017 by the Iraqi military in a US-backed campaign that left the city only partially in rubble, unlike so many of the fully rubblized cities in the region. In the Obama years, McMaster became the leader of a task force in Afghanistan that "sought to root out the rampant corruption that had taken hold" in the American-backed government there, an effort that would prove a dismal failure.

Marine General Mattis led Task Force 58 into southern Afghanistan in the invasion of 2001, establishing the "first conventional US military presence in the country." He repeated the act in Iraq in 2003, leading the 1st Marine Division in the invasion of that country. He was involved in the taking of the Iraqi capital, Baghdad, in 2003; in the fierce fighting for and partial destruction of the city of Fallujah in 2004; and, in that same year, the bombing of what turned out to be a wedding party, not insurgents, near the Syrian border. ("How many people go to the middle of the desert . . . to hold a wedding eighty miles from the nearest civilization?" was his response to the news.) In 2010, he was made head of US Central Command, overseeing the wars in both Iraq and Afghanistan until 2011 when he urged the

Obama administration to launch a "dead of night" operation to take out an Iranian oil refinery or power plant, his idea of an appropriate response to Iran's role in Iraq. His proposal was rejected, and he was "retired" from his command five months early. In other words, he lost his chance to set off yet another never-ending American war in the Middle East. He is known for his "Mattisisms" like this piece of advice to Marines in Iraq in 2003: "Be polite, be professional, but have a plan to kill everybody you meet."

Retired Marine General John Kelly was assistant division commander in Iraq under Mattis, who personally promoted him to brigadier general on the battlefield. (The present head of the Joint Chiefs of Staff, General Joe Dunford, was an officer in the same division at the same time and all three reportedly remain friends.) Though Kelly had a second tour of duty in Iraq, he never fought in Afghanistan. Tragically, however, one of his sons (who had also fought in Fallujah in 2004) died there after stepping on an improvised explosive device in 2010.

McMaster was among the earliest figures in the Pentagon to begin speaking of the country's post–9/11 wars as "generational" (that is, never-ending). In 2014, he said, "If you think this war against our way of life is over because some of the self-appointed opinion-makers and chattering class grow 'war weary,' because they want to be out of Iraq or Afghanistan, you are mistaken. This enemy is dedicated to our destruction. He will fight us for generations, and the conflict will move through various phases as it has since 9/11."

In short, you could hardly pick three men more viscerally connected to the American way of war, less capable of seriously reassessing what they have lived through, or more fully identified with the failures of the war on terror, especially the conflicts in Iraq and Afghanistan. When it comes to the "rubble" of American generalship in these years, Mattis, McMaster, and Kelly would certainly be at the top of anyone's list.

They are the ultimate survivors of a system that at its upper levels is not known, even in the best of times, for promoting original, outside-the-box thinkers. They are, in other words, the ultimate four-star conformists because that's the character trait you need to make it to generalship in the US military. (Original thinkers and critics never seem to make it past the rank of colonel.)

And as their "new" Trump-era Afghan policy indicates, when faced with their wars and what to do about them, their answer is invariably some version of more of the same (despite the usual, by-now-predictable results).

All Hail the Generals!

In these years, America's generals have failed everywhere except in one place, and that just happens to be the only place that truly matters. Call Afghanistan a "stalemate" as often as you want, all these years after the US loosed the power of "the finest fighting force the world has ever known," the Taliban are ascendant in that benighted land and that's the definition of failure, no matter how you tote things up. Trump's generals have indeed been losers in that country, as they and others have been in Iraq, Somalia, Yemen, Libya, and someday will be, undoubtedly, in Syria (no matter what immediate victories they might chalk up). In only one place did their generalship work effectively; in only one place have they truly succeeded; in only one place could they now conceivably proclaim "victory at last!"

That place is, of course, Washington, DC, where they are indeed the last men standing and, in Trumpian terms, absolute winners.

In Washington, their generalship has been anything but rubble. It's always been another kind of more—more of whatever they wanted, from money to surges to ever-greater power and authority. In Washington, they've been the winners ever since President George W. Bush launched his Global War on Terror.

What they couldn't do in Baghdad, Kabul, Tripoli, or anywhere else across the Greater Middle East and Africa, they've done impressively in our nation's capital. In years when they unsuccessfully brought the full power of the greatest arsenal on the planet to bear on enemies whose weaponry cost the price of a pizza, they continued to rake in billions of dollars in Washington. In fact, it's reasonable to argue that the losing conflicts in the war on terror were necessary prerequisites to winning budgetary battles in that city. Those never-ending conflicts—and the fear of (Islamic) terrorism heavily promoted by the national security state—have driven funding success to staggering levels in the nation's capital, perhaps the single issue on which Republicans and Democrats have seen eye to eye in this period.

In this context, Donald Trump's decision to surround himself with "his" generals has simply brought this reality more fully into focus. He's made it clear why the term "deep state," often used by critics of American war and national security policies, inadequately describes the situation in Washington in this century. That term brings up images of a hidden state-within-a-state that controls the rest of the government in some conspiratorial fashion. The reality in Washington today is nothing like that. Despite both its trove of secrets and its desire to cast a shadow of secrecy over government operations, the national security state hasn't exactly been lurking in the shadows in these years.

In Washington, whatever the Constitution may say about civilian control of the military, the generals—at present—control the civilians and the deep state has become the all-too-visible state. In this context, one thing is clear, whether you're talking about the country's panoply of "intelligence" agencies or the Pentagon, failure is the new success.

And for all of this, one thing continues to be essential: those "generational struggles" in distant lands. If you want to see how this works in a nutshell, consider a single line from a recent piece on the Afghan War by *New York Times* reporter Rod Nordland. "Even before the president's [Afghan] speech, the American military and Afghan leaders were laying long-term plans," Nordland pointed out, and added in passing, "The American military has a $6.5-billion plan to make the Afghan Air Force self-sufficient and end its overreliance on American air power by 2023."

Think for a moment about that relatively modest part (a mere $6.5 billion!) of the military's latest plans for a more-of-the-same future in Afghanistan. As a start, we're already talking about six more years of a war that began in October 2001, was essentially an extension of a previous conflict fought there from 1979 to 1989, and is already the longest war in American history. In other words, the depiction of a "generational struggle" is anything but an exaggeration.

Recall as well that, in January 2008, Brigadier General Jay Lindell, then-commander of the Combined Air Power Transition Force in Afghanistan, announced an eight-year American plan that would leave the Afghan Air Force fully staffed, supplied, trained, and "self-sufficient" by 2015. In 2015, Rod Nordland would check out that air force and find it in a "woeful state" of near ruin.

So in 2023, if that full $6.5 billion has indeed been invested in—perhaps the more fitting phrase might be "squandered on"—the Afghan Air Force, one thing is a given: it will still not be "self-sufficient." After all, so many years later, with more than $65 billion already appropriated by Congress and spent on the training of the Afghan security forces, they are taking terrible casualties, experiencing horrendous desertion rates, filled with "ghost" personnel, and are anything but self-sufficient. Why imagine a different fate for that country's air force for a mere $6.5 billion more?

In America's war on terror, such things should be considered tales foretold, even as the losing generals of those losing wars strut their stuff in Washington. Elsewhere on the planet, the US military's plans for 2020, 2023, and beyond will undoubtedly prove to be yet more landmarks on a highway to failure—only in Washington do such plans invariably work out. Only in Washington does more of the same turn out to be the ultimate formula for success. Our losing wars, it seems, are a necessary backdrop for the ultimate winning war in our nation's capital. So, all hail America's generals! Mission accomplished!

Failure Is the New Success

It was bloody and brutal, a true generational struggle, but give them credit: in the end, they won when so many lost.

James Comey was axed. Sean Spicer went down in a heap of ashes. Anthony Scaramucci crashed and burned instantaneously. Reince Priebus hung on for dear life but was finally canned. Seven months in, Steve Bannon got the old heave-ho and soon after, his minion, Sebastian Gorka, was unceremoniously shoved out the White House door, too. In a downpour of potential conflicts of interest and scandal, Carl

Icahn bowed out. Tom Price was cashiered. And so it's gone in the Trump administration.

Except for the generals, the last men standing. They did it. They took the high ground in Washington and so far they've held it with remarkable panache. Three of them, National Security Advisor Lieutenant General H. R. McMaster, Secretary of Defense and retired marine general James Mattis, and former head of the Department of Homeland Security, now White House chief of staff retired marine general John Kelly stand alone—except for President Trump's own family members—at the pinnacle of power in Washington.

Those three generals from America's losing wars are, at least for now, triumphant. One of them is the ultimate gatekeeper when it comes to who sees the president. All three influence his thoughts and speeches. They are the "civilians" who control the military and American war policy. They, and they alone, have made the president go against his deepest urges, as he admitted in his address to the nation on the war in Afghanistan. ("My original instinct was to pull out and historically I like following my instincts.") They've convinced him to release the military (and the CIA) from significant oversight in pursuing their wars as they wish across the Greater Middle East, Africa, and now the Philippines. They even convinced him to surround their future actions in a penumbra of secrecy.

SEVEN

Bombing the Rubble

If you want to know where President Donald Trump came from, if you want to trace the long winding road (or escalator) that brought him to the Oval Office, don't look to reality TV or Twitter or even the rise of the alt-right. Look someplace far more improbable: Iraq.

Donald Trump may have been born in New York City. He may have grown to manhood amid his hometown's real estate wars. He may have gone no further than Atlantic City, New Jersey, to casino-ize the world and create those magical golden letters that would become the essence of his brand. He may have made an even more magical leap to television without leaving home, turning "You're fired!" into a household phrase. Still, his presidency is another matter entirely. It's an immigrant: it arrived, fully radicalized, with its bouffant comb-over and eternal tan, from Iraq.

Despite his denials that he was ever in favor of the 2003 invasion of that country, Donald Trump is a president made by war. His elevation to the highest office in the land is inconceivable without that invasion, which began in glory and ended (if ended it ever did) in infamy. He's the president of a land remade by war in ways its people have yet to absorb. Admittedly, he avoided war in his personal life entirely. He was a Vietnam no-show. And yet he's the president that war brought home. Think of him not as President Blowhard but as President Blowback.

"Go Massive. Sweep It All Up"

To grasp this, a little escalator ride down memory lane is necessary— all the way back to 9/11, to, that is, the grimmest day in our recent history. There's no other way to recall just how gloriously it all began than amid the rubble. You could, if you wanted, choose the moment three days after the World Trade Center towers collapsed when, bull-horn in hand, President George W. Bush ascended part of that rubble pile in downtown Manhattan, put his arm around a firefighter, and shouted into a bullhorn, "I can hear you! The rest of the world hears you! . . . And the people who knocked these buildings down will hear all of us soon."

The genesis of Donald Trump's presidency, however, can be sit-uated in an even earlier moment—at a Pentagon partially in ruins thanks to hijacked American Airlines Flight 77. There, only five hours after the attack, Secretary of Defense Donald Rumsfeld, al-ready aware that the destruction around him was probably Osama bin Laden's responsibility, ordered his aides (according to notes one of them took) to begin planning for a retaliatory strike against . . . yes, Saddam Hussein's Iraq. His exact words: "Go massive. Sweep it all up. Things related and not." And swept almost instantly into the giant dustbin of what would become the Global War on Terror (or GWOT), as ordered, would be something completely unrelated to 9/11—not that the Bush administration ever admitted that. It was, however, in-timately related to the deepest dreams of the men (and woman) who oversaw foreign policy in the Bush years: the elimination of Iraq's autocratic ruler, Saddam Hussein.

Yes, there was bin Laden to be dealt with and the Taliban and Af-ghanistan, too, but that was small change, almost instantly taken care of with some air power, CIA dollars delivered to Afghan warlords, and a modest number of American troops. Within months, Afghani-stan had been "liberated," bin Laden had fled the country, the Taliban had laid down their arms, and that was that. (Who in Washington then imagined that, more than fifteen years later, a new administration would be dealing with a request from yet another US military commander in that country for yet more troops to shore up a failing war there?)

Within months the decks seemed clear to pursue what George W. Bush, Dick Cheney & Co. saw as their destiny, as the key to America's future imperial glory: the taking down of the Iraqi dictator. That, as Rumsfeld indicated at the Pentagon that day in the chaos of 9/11, was always where they were truly focused. It was what some of them had dreamed of since the moment, in the first Gulf War of 1990–1991, when President George H. W. Bush stopped the troops short of a march on Baghdad and left Hussein, America's former ally and later Hitlerian nemesis, in power.

The invasion of March 2003 was, they had no doubt, to be an unparalleled moment in America's history as a global power—as it would indeed turn out to be, even if not in the way they imagined. The military that George W. Bush would call "the greatest force for human liberation the world has ever known" was slated to liberate Iraq via a miraculous, high-tech, shock-and-awe campaign that the world would never forget. This time, unlike in 1991, its troops would enter Baghdad, Saddam would go down in flames, and it would all happen without the help of the militaries of twenty-eight other countries.

It would instead be an act of imperial loneliness befitting the last superpower on Planet Earth. The Iraqi people would naturally greet us as liberators and we would set up a long-term garrison state in the oil heartlands of the Middle East. At the moment the invasion was launched, in fact, the Pentagon already had drawn up plans for the building of four permanent mega-bases (initially endearingly labeled "enduring camps") in Iraq, on which thousands of US troops could hunker down for an eternity. At the peak of the occupation, there were more than five hundred bases, ranging from tiny combat outposts to ones the size of small American towns. Many were transformed after 2011 into the ghost towns of a dream gone mad until a few were reoccupied by US troops in the battle against the Islamic State.

Following the friendly occupation of now-democratic (and grateful) Iraq, the hostile Syria of the al-Assad family would naturally find itself between a hammer and an anvil (that is, between American-garrisoned Iraq and Israel), and the fundamentalist Iranian regime, after more than two decades of implacable anti-American hostility, would be done for. The neocon quip of that moment was: "Everyone wants to go to Baghdad. Real men want to go to Tehran." Soon enough—it was inevitable— Washington would dominate the Greater Middle East from Pakistan to North Africa in a way no great power ever had. It would be the beginning of a *Pax Americana* moment on Planet Earth that would stretch on for generations to come.

Such was the dream. Now, let's remember the reality, the one that led to a looted capital, Saddam's army tossed out on the streets jobless to join the uprisings to come, a bitter set of insurgencies (Sunni and Shia), civil war (and local ethnic cleansing), a society-wide reconstruction program overseen by American warrior corporations linked to the Pentagon resulting in vast boondoggle projects that achieved little and reconstructed nothing, prisons from hell (including Abu Ghraib) that bred yet more insurgents, and finally, years down the line, the Islamic State and the present version of American war now taking place in Syria as well as Iraq.

Meanwhile, as our new president said in a speech to Congress, literally trillions of dollars that might have been spent on actual American security (broadly understood) were squandered on a failed military project that left our domestic infrastructure in disarray. All in all, it was quite a record. In return for the destruction of part of the Pentagon and a section of downtown Manhattan that was turned to rubble, the United States would set off a series of wars, conflicts, insurgencies, and burgeoning terror movements that would transform significant parts of the Greater Middle East into failed or failing states, and their cities and towns, startling numbers of them, into so much rubble.

Once upon a time, all of this seemed so distant to Americans as President Bush quickly urged citizens to show their patriotism not by sacrificing or mobilizing or even joining the military, but by visiting Disney World and reestablishing patterns of pre–9/11 consumption as if nothing had happened ("Get down to Disney World in Florida. Take your families and enjoy life, the way we want it to be enjoyed").

And indeed, personal consumption would rise significantly that October 2001.

The other side of the glory-to-come, in those years of remarkable peace in the United States, was to be the passivity of a demobilized populace that (except for periodic thank-yous to its military) would have little to do with the far-off wars, which were to be left to the pros, even if fought in their name.

That, of course, was the dream. Reality proved to be another matter entirely.

Invading America

In the end, a victory-less permanent war across the Greater Middle East did indeed come home. There was all the new hardware of war—the StingRays, the MRAPs, the drones, and so on—that migrated homewards, and that was the least of it. There was the militarization of America's police forces, not to speak of the rise of the national security state to the status of an unofficial fourth branch of government. Home, too, came the post–9/11 fears, the vague but unnerving sense that somewhere in the world strange and incomprehensible aliens practicing an eerie religion were out to get us, that some of them had near-super powers that even the world's greatest military couldn't crush, and that their potential acts of terror were Topeka's greatest danger. It mattered little that actual Islamic terror was among the least of the dangers Americans faced in their daily lives.

All of this reached its conclusion (at least thus far) in Donald Trump. In its own strange way, the Trump phenomenon should be seen as the culmination of the invasion of 2003 brought home *bigly*. His would be a shock-and-awe election campaign in which he would "decapitate" his rivals one by one. The New York real estate, hotel, and casino magnate who had long swum comfortably in the waters of the liberal elite when he needed to and had next to nothing to do with America's heartland would be as alien to its inhabitants as the US military was to Iraqis when it invaded. And yet he would indeed launch his own invasion of that heartland from his private jet with its gold-plated bathroom fixtures, sweeping up all the fears that had been gathering in this country since 9/11 (nurtured by both politicians and national security state officials for their own benefit). And those fears would ring a bell so loud in that heartland that they would carry him into the White House. In November 2016, he took Baghdad, USA, in high style.

In this context, the invasion of Iraq, in some pretzeled form, seemed to have blown back on America.

Like the neocons of the Bush administration, Donald Trump had long dreamed of his moment of imperial glory, and as in Afghanistan and again in Iraq in 2001 and 2003, when it arrived on November 8, 2016, it couldn't have seemed more glorious. We know of these dreams of his because, for one thing, only six days after Mitt Romney lost to Barack Obama in the 2012 election campaign, The Donald first tried to trademark the old Reagan-inspired slogan, "Make America Great Again."

Like George W. and Dick Cheney, Trump was intent on invading and occupying the oil heartlands of the planet which, in 2003, had indeed been Iraq. By 2015–2016, however, the United States had entered the energy heartlands sweepstakes, as fracking and other advanced methods of extracting fossil fuels turned the country into "Saudi America." Add to this Trump's plans to further fossil-fuelize the continent and you certainly have a worthy competitor to the Middle East. In a sense, it might be said, adapting his campaign description of what he would have preferred to do in Iraq, that Donald Trump wants to "keep" our oil.

Like the US military in 2003, he, too, arrived on the scene with plans to turn his country of choice into a garrison state. Almost the first words out of his mouth on entering the presidential race in June 2015 involved a promise to protect Americans from Mexican "rapists" by building an impregnable "great wall" on the country's southern border. From this claim he never strayed even when it became apparent that, from the Coast Guard to airport security to the Federal Emergency Management Agency, as president he would be cutting into genuine security measures in order to build his "great wall."

It's clear, however, that his urge to create a garrison state far surpassed a literal wall. It included the build-up of the military to unprecedented heights, as well as the bolstering of the regular police, and above all of the border police. Beyond that lay the urge to wall Americans off in every way possible. His fervently publicized immigration policies (less new, in reality, than they seemed) should be thought of as part of a project to construct another kind of great wall, a conceptual one whose message to the rest of the world was striking: You are not welcome or wanted here. Don't come. Don't visit.

All of this was, in turn, grafted onto the many irrational fears that had been gathering like storm clouds for so many years, and that Trump (and his alt-right companions) swept into the already looted heartland of the country. In the process, he unleashed a brand of hate (including shootings, mosque burnings, a raft of bomb threats, and a rise in hate groups, especially anti-Muslim ones) that, historically, was all American, but was nonetheless remarkable in its intensity in our present moment.

Combined with his highly publicized "Muslim travel bans" and prominently publicized acts of hate, the Trump walling-in of America quickly hit home. A drop in foreigners who wanted to visit this country was almost instantly apparent as the warning signs of a tourism "Trump slump" registered, business travel bookings took a quick $185 million hit, and the travel industry predicted worse to come.

This is evidently what "America First" actually means: a country walled off and walled in. Indeed, the road traveled from 2003 to 2017 was from sole global superpower to potential super-pariah.

In the United States, the bedraggled land whose infrastructure recently was given a D+ grade on a "report card" issued by the American Society of Civil Engineers, Donald Trump promises a trillion-dollar infrastructure program to rebuild America's highways, tunnels, bridges, airports, and the like. If it actually comes about, it will most certainly be handed over to some of the same warrior corporations that reconstructed Iraq (and other corporate entities like them), functionally guaranteeing an American version of that budget-draining boondoggle.

And one more thing: the blowback wars out of which Donald Trump and the present fear-gripped garrison state of America arose have yet to end. In fact, just as under Presidents George W. Bush and Barack Obama, under President Trump, it seems they never will. So whatever the blowback may have been, we've only seen its beginning. It's bound to last for years to come.

There's just one phrase that could adequately sum all this up: Mission accomplished!

Precision Warfare? Don't Make Me Laugh

It was supposed to be twenty-first-century war, American style: precise beyond imagining; smart bombs; drones capable of taking out a carefully identified and tracked human being just about anywhere on Earth; special operations raids so pinpoint-accurate that they would represent a triumph of modern military science. Everything "networked." It was to be a glorious dream of limited destruction combined with unlimited power and success. In reality, it would prove to be a nightmare of the first order.

If a single word might summarize American war-making in this last decade and a half, it could be rubble. It's been a painfully apt term since September 11, 2001. But to catch the essence of such war in this century, two new words might also be useful: rubblize and rubblization.

In 2017, another major city in Iraq was officially "liberated" from the militants of the Islamic State. However, the results of the US-backed Iraqi military campaign to retake Mosul, that country's second-largest city, don't fit any ordinary definition of triumph or victory. The campaign began in October 2016 and, at nine months and counting, has been longer than the World War II battle of Stalingrad. Week after week, in street-to-street fighting, with US airstrikes repeatedly called in on neighborhoods still filled with terrified Mosulites, unknown but potentially staggering numbers of civilians have died. More than a million people—yes, you read that figure correctly—were uprooted from their homes, and major portions of the western half of the city they fled, including its ancient historic sections, have been rubblized.

This should be the definition of victory as defeat, success as disaster. It's also a pattern. It's been the essential story of the American war on terror since President George W. Bush unleashed American air power on Afghanistan in the month after the 9/11 attacks. That first air campaign began what has increasingly come to look like a plan for the full-scale rubblization of significant parts of the Greater Middle East.

By not simply going after the crew who committed those attacks but deciding to take down the Taliban, occupy Afghanistan, and in 2003, invade Iraq, the Bush administration opened the proverbial can of worms in that vast region. An imperial urge to overthrow Iraqi ruler Saddam Hussein, who had once been Washington's guy in the Middle East only to become its mortal enemy (and who had nothing whatsoever to do with 9/11), proved one of the fatal miscalculations of that imperial era.

So, too, did the deeply engrained fantasy of Bush administration officials that they controlled a high-tech, precision military that could project power in ways no other nation on the planet or in history ever had. With Iraq occupied and garrisoned (Korea-style) for generations to come, his top officials assumed that they would next take down fundamentalist Iran and other hostile regimes in the region. (Hence, the particular irony of the present Iranian ascendancy in Iraq.) In the pursuit of such fantasies of global power, the Bush administration, in effect, punched a devastating hole in the oil heartlands of the Middle East. In the acerbic imagery of Abu Mussa, head of the Arab League at the time, the United States chose to drive straight through "the gates of hell."

Rubblizing the Greater Middle East

Since 9/11, parts of an expanding swath of the planet—from Pakistan's borderlands in South Asia to Libya in North Africa—were catastrophically unsettled. Tiny groups of Islamic terrorists multiplied exponentially into both local and transnational organizations, spreading across the region with the help of the anger American "precision" warfare stirred among helpless civilian populations. States began to totter or fail. Countries essentially collapsed, delivering a tide of refugees to the world, as year after year, the US military, its special operations forces, and the CIA were increasingly deployed in one fashion or another in one country after another.

Though in case after case the results were visibly disastrous, like so many addicts, the three post–9/11 administrations in Washington proved incapable of drawing the obvious conclusions and instead continued to do more of the same (with modest adjustments of one sort of another). The results, unsurprisingly enough, were similarly disappointing or disastrous.

Despite the doubts about such a form of global warfare that candidate Trump raised during the 2016 election campaign, the process has only escalated in his presidency so far. Washington, it seems, just can't help itself in its drive to pursue this version of war in all its grim imprecision to its increasingly imprecise but predictably destructive conclusions. Worse yet, if the leading military and political figures in Washington have their way, none of this may end in our lifetime.

If anything, so many years after it was launched, the war on terror shows every sign of continuing to expand and rubblization is increasingly the name of the game. Here's a very partial tally sheet on the subject:

In addition to Mosul, a number of Iraq's other major cities and towns—including Ramadi and Fallujah—have been reduced to rubble. Across the border in Syria, where a brutal civil war has been raging since 2011, numerous cities and towns, from Homs to parts of Aleppo, have essentially been destroyed. Raqqa, the "capital" of the self-proclaimed Islamic State, is now under siege. It, too, will be "liberated" sooner or later—that is to say, destroyed in whole or in part.

As in Mosul, Fallujah, and Ramadi, American planes have been striking ISIS positions in the urban heart of Raqqa and killing civilians, evidently in sizeable numbers, while rubblizing parts of the city. And such activities have in recent years only been spreading. In distant Libya, for instance, the city of Sirte is in ruins after a similar struggle involving local forces, American air power, and ISIS militants. In Yemen, for the last two years the Saudis have been conducting a never-ending air campaign (with American support), significantly aimed at the civilian population; they have, that is, been rubblizing that country, and so paving the way for a devastating famine and a horrific cholera epidemic that can't be checked, given the condition of that impoverished, embattled land.

Only recently, this sort of destruction has spread for the first time beyond the Greater Middle East and parts of Africa. In late May 2017, on the island of Mindanao in the southern Philippines, local Muslim rebels identified with ISIS took Marawi City. Since they moved in, much of its population of 200,000 has been displaced and almost two months later the rebels still hold parts of the city and are engaged in Mosul-style urban warfare with the Filipino military (backed by US special operations advisers). In the process, the area has reportedly also suffered Mosul-style rubblization.

In most of these rubblized cities and the regions around them, even when "victory" is declared, worse yet is in sight. In Iraq, for instance, with the "caliphate" of Abu Bakr al-Baghdadi now being dismantled, ISIS nevertheless remains a genuinely threatening guerilla force, the Sunni and Shiite communities (including armed Shiite militias) show little sign of coming together, and in the north of the country the Kurds are threatening to declare an independent state. So, fighting of various sorts is essentially guaranteed and the possibility of Iraq turning into a full-scale failed state or several devastated mini-states remains all too real, even as the Trump administration is reportedly pushing Congress for permission to construct and occupy new "temporary" military bases and other facilities in the country (and in neighboring Syria).

Worse yet, across the Greater Middle East, "reconstruction" is basically not even a concept. There's simply no money for it. Oil prices remain deeply depressed and, from Libya and Yemen to Iraq and Syria, countries are either too poor or too divided to begin the reconstruction of much of anything. Nor—and this is a given—will Donald Trump's America be launching the war on terror equivalent of a post–World War II–style Marshall Plan for the region.

And even if it did, the record of the post-9/11 years already shows that in both Iraq and Afghanistan the highly militarized American version of "reconstruction" or "nation building" via crony corporations has been one of the great scams of our time. More American taxpayer dollars have been poured into reconstruction efforts in Afghanistan alone than went into the whole of the Marshall Plan, and it's painfully obvious how effective that proved to be.

Of course, as in Syria's civil war, Washington is hardly solely responsible for all the devastation in the region. ISIS itself has been a remarkably brutal killing machine with its own impressive record of urban rubblization. Yet most of the destruction was triggered, at least, by the militarized ambitions of the Bush administration in its response to 9/11 (and ended up playing out something like Osama bin Laden's dream scenario). Don't forget that al-Qaeda in Iraq, ISIS's predecessor, was a creature of the American invasion and occupation of that country, and that ISIS itself was essentially formed in an American military prison camp in Iraq in which its future caliph was confined.

In the first months of the Trump administration, the United States essentially decided on a new mini-surge of troops and air power in Afghanistan; deployed there for the first time the largest non-nuclear weapon in its arsenal; promised the Saudis more support in their war in Yemen; increased air strikes and special operations activities in Somalia; began preparing for a new military presence in Libya; increased ground forces and eased the rules for air strikes in civilian areas of Iraq and elsewhere; and sent special operators and other personnel in rising numbers into both Iraq and Syria.

No matter the president, the ante only seems to go up when it comes to the war on terror, a war of imprecision that has helped uproot record numbers of people with the usual predictable results: the further spread of terror groups, the further destabilization of state structures, rising numbers of displaced and dead civilians, and the rubblization of expanding parts of the planet.

While no one would deny the destructive potential of great imperial powers historically, the American empire of destruction may be unique: at the height of its military strength, it has been utterly incapable of translating its power advantage into anything but rubblization.

Living in the Rubble, a Short History of the Twenty-First Century

Let me speak personally here, since I live in the remarkably protected and peaceful heart of that empire of destruction and in the very city where it all began. What eternally puzzles me is the inability of those who run our imperial machinery to absorb what's actually happened since 9/11 and draw any reasonable conclusions from it. After all, so much of what I've been describing seems, at this point, dismally obvious.

If anything, the "generational" nature of the war on terror and the way it became a permanent war *of* terror should by now seem too self-evident for discussion. And yet, despite whatever he said on the campaign trail, President Trump promptly appointed to key positions the very generals who have long been immersed in fighting America's wars and are clearly ready to do more of the same. Why in the world anyone, even those generals, should imagine that such an approach could result in anything more "successful" is beyond me.

In many ways, rubblization has been at the heart of this whole process, starting with the moment of 9/11 itself. After all, the very point of those attacks was to turn the symbols of American power—the Pentagon (military power); the World Trade Center (financial power); and the Capitol or some other Washington edifice (political power), as the hijacked plane that crashed in a field in Pennsylvania was undoubtedly heading there—into so much rubble. In the process, thousands of innocent civilians were slaughtered.

In some ways, much of the rubblization of the Greater Middle East in recent years could be thought of as, however unconsciously, a campaign of vengeance for the horror and insult of the air assaults on that September morning in 2001, which pulverized the tallest towers of my hometown. Ever since, American war has, in a sense, involved paying Osama bin Laden back in kind, but on a staggering scale. In Afghanistan, Iraq, and elsewhere, a shocking but passing single moment for Americans has become everyday life for whole populations, and innocents have died in numbers that would add up to so many World Trade Centers piled atop each other.

I was in New York City on that day. I experienced the shock of the attacks and the smell of those burning buildings. A friend of mine saw a hijacked plane hitting one of the towers, and another biked into the smoke-filled area looking for his daughter. I went down to the site of the attacks with my own daughter within days and wandered the nearby streets, catching glimpses of those giant shards of destroyed buildings.

In the phrase of that moment, in the wake of 9/11 "everything changed" and indeed it did. I felt it. Who didn't? I noted the sense of fear rising nationally and the repetitious ceremonies across the country in which Americans hailed themselves as the planet's most exceptional victims, survivors, and future victors. In those post–9/11 weeks, I became increasingly aware of how a growing sense of shock and a desire for vengeance among the populace was freeing Bush administration officials, who had for years been dreaming about making the "lone superpower" omnipotent in a historically unprecedented way, to act more or less as they wished.

As for myself, I was overcome by a sense that the period to follow would be the worst of my life, far worse than the Vietnam era, the last time I had been truly mobilized politically. And of one thing I was certain: things would not go well. I had an urge to do something, though no idea what.

In early October 2001, the Bush administration unleashed its air power on Afghanistan, a campaign that, in a sense, would never end but simply spread across the Greater Middle East. At that moment, someone emailed me an article by Tamim Ansary, an Afghan who had been in the United States for years but had continued to follow events in his country of birth.

His piece, which appeared on the website *Counterpunch*, would prove prescient indeed, especially since it had been written in mid-September, just days after 9/11. As Ansary noted, Americans were already threatening—in a phrase adopted from the Vietnam War era—to bomb Afghanistan "back to the Stone Age." What purpose, he wondered, could possibly be served by such a bombing campaign since, as he put it, "new bombs would only stir the rubble of earlier bombs"? As he pointed out, Afghanistan, then largely ruled by the grim Taliban, had essentially been turned into rubble years before in the proxy war the Soviets and Americans fought there until the Red Army limped home in defeat in 1989. The rubble that was already Afghanistan only increased in the brutal civil war that followed. And in the years before 2001, little had been rebuilt. So, as Ansary made clear, the United States was about to launch its air power for the first time in the twenty-first century against a country of ruins and in ruins.

From such an act, he predicted disaster. And so it would prove to be. At the time, something about that image of air strikes on rubble stunned me, in part because it felt both horrifying and true, in part because it seemed such an ominous signal of what might lie in our future, and in part because nothing like Ansary's article could then be found in the mainstream news or in any kind of debate about how to respond to 9/11 (of which there was essentially none). Impulsively, I emailed his piece out with a note of my own to friends and relatives, something I had never done before. That, as it turned out, would be the start of what became an ever-expanding no-name listserv and, a little more than a year later, *TomDispatch*.

A Plutocracy of the Rubble?

So, the first word to fully catch my attention and set me in motion in the post–9/11 era was "rubble." It's sad that, so many years later, Americans are still obsessively afraid for themselves, a fear that has helped fund and build a national security state of staggering dimensions. On the other hand, remarkably few of us have any grasp of the endless 9/11–style experiences our military has so imprecisely delivered to the world. The bombs may be smart, but the acts couldn't be dumber.

In this country, there is no real feeling of responsibility for the spread of terrorism, the crumbling of states, the destruction of lives and livelihoods, the tidal flow of refugees, and the rubblization of some of the planet's great cities. There's no reasonable assessment of the true nature and effects of American warfare abroad: its imprecision, its idiocy, its devastation. In this peaceful land, it's hard to imagine the true impact of the imprecision of war, American style. Given the way things are going, it's easy enough, however, to imagine the scenario of Tamim Ansary writ large in the Trump years and those to follow: Americans continuing to bomb the rubble they had such a hand in creating across the Greater Middle East.

And yet distant imperial wars do have a way of coming home, and not just in the form of new surveillance techniques, or drones flying over "the homeland," or the full-scale militarization of police forces. Without those disastrous, never-ending wars, I suspect that the election of Donald Trump would have been unlikely. And while he will not loose such "precision" warfare on the homeland itself, his project (and that of the congressional Republicans)—from health care to the environment—is visibly aimed at rubblizing our society. If he were capable, he would certainly create a plutocracy of the rubble in a world where ruins are increasingly the norm.

The Globalization of Misery

In mid-October 2016, the US-backed Iraqi Army first launched an offensive to retake Mosul from the militants of the Islamic State. Relatively small numbers of ISIS fighters had captured it in mid-2014 when the previous version of the Iraqi military (into which the United States had poured more than $25 billion) collapsed ignominiously and fled, abandoning much of its weaponry and even uniforms along the way. It was in Mosul's Great Mosque that the existence of the Islamic State was first triumphantly proclaimed by its "caliph," Abu Bakr al-Baghdadi.

On the initial day of the offensive to recapture the city, the Pentagon was already congratulating the Iraqi military for being "ahead of schedule" in a campaign that was expected to "take weeks or even months." Little did its planners—who had been announcing its prospective start for nearly a year—know. A week later, everything was still "proceeding according to our plan," claimed then–secretary of defense Ashton Carter. By the end of January 2017, after one hundred days of fierce fighting, the eastern part of the city, divided by the Tigris River, was more or less back in government hands and it had, according to *New York Times* reporters on the scene, been "spared the wholesale destruction inflicted on other Iraqi cities" like Ramadi and Fallujah, even though those residents who hadn't fled were reportedly "scratching out a primitive existence, deprived of electricity, running water and other essential city services."

And that was the good news. More than one hundred days later, Iraqi troops continue to edge their way through embattled western Mosul, with parts of it, including the treacherous warren of streets in its Old City, still in the hands of ISIS militants amid continuing bitter building-to-building fighting. American air power has repeatedly been called in big time, while Islamic State fighters have employed countless bomb-laden suicide vehicles and even small drones in defense of their positions in the battle-scarred city as civilian deaths soared and hundreds of thousands of its inhabitants were left increasingly desperate and hungry.

After so many months of unending battle in that single city, perhaps it shouldn't have been surprising that Mosul receded from the news, even as at least half a million Iraqis were displaced, and the Iraqi military suffered grievous losses.

Despite initial claims that the Iraqi military (and the US Air Force) were taking great care to avoid destruction as much as possible in an urban landscape filled with civilians, the rules of engagement changed as the battle went on and in the end significant swaths of Iraq's second-largest city were left in ruins like so many other cities and towns in Iraq and Syria.

The Disappearance of Mosul

At a moment when Donald Trump made headlines daily with almost any random thing he said, the fate of Mosul didn't even qualify as a major news story. What happened in that city, however, was no minor thing. It matters on this increasingly small planet of ours.

What's to come is also, unfortunately, reasonably predictable. After nine months, the grim Islamic State in Mosul was destroyed, but so was much of the city in a region that continues to be rubblized. The announcement of its "liberation" made headlines, but soon after Mosul once again disappeared from our American world and worries. Yet that is undoubtedly only the beginning of the story in a world in crisis.

In Mosul alone, untold numbers of people whose fathers, mothers, grandparents, children, friends, and relatives were slaughtered in the Iraqi Army's offensive or murdered by ISIS were themselves left homeless, often without possessions, jobs, or communities in the midst of the once familiar places that had been transformed into rubble. Mosul now lacks an airport, a railroad station, and a university—all destroyed in the recent fighting. Initial estimates suggest that its rebuilding will cost billions of dollars over many years. And it's just one of many cities in such a state.

In other words, the Iraqis, the Syrians, the Yemenis, the Libyans, the Afghans, and others are likely, in the end, to find themselves alone in the ruins of their worlds with remarkably little recourse. With that in mind and given the record of those last fourteen years, how exactly do you imagine that things will turn out for the inhabitants of Mosul, or Ramadi, or Fallujah, or cities yet to be destroyed? What new movements, ethnic struggles, and terror outfits will emerge from such a nightmare?

Where Is Globalization Now That We Need It?

To frame things slightly differently, let me ask another question: What ever happened to "globalization" and the endless media attention that was once paid to it? Not so very long ago we were being assured that this planet was binding itself into a remarkably tight knot of interconnectedness that was going to amaze us all. As Thomas Friedman of the *New York Times* put it in 1996, we were seeing "the integration of free markets, nation-states, and information technologies to a degree never before witnessed, in a way that is enabling individuals, corporations, and countries to reach around the world farther, faster, deeper, and cheaper than ever." All of this was to be fed and led by the United States, the last remaining superpower, and as a result, the global "playing field" would miraculously "be leveled" on a planet becoming a mosaic of Pizza Huts, iMacs, and Lexuses.

Who of a certain age doesn't remember those years after the Soviet Union imploded when we all suddenly found ourselves in a single-superpower world? It was a moment when, thanks to vaunted technological advances, it seemed blindingly clear to the cognoscenti that this was going to be a single-everything planet. We were all about to be absorbed into a "single market for goods, capital, and commercial services" from which, despite the worries of naysayers, "almost everyone" stood "to gain." In a new world not of multiple superpowers but of multiple "supermarkets," we were likely to become both more democratic and more capitalistic by the year as an interlocking set of transnational corporate players, nations, and peoples, unified by a singularly interwoven set of communication systems (representing nothing short of an information revolution) would triumph, while poverty, that eternal plague of humanity, would lose out big time. Everything would be connected on what was to be, for the first time, a "flattened" planet.

That's not exactly the planet we're now on. Instead, whatever processes have been at work, the result has been record numbers of billionaires, record levels of inequality, and refugees in numbers not seen since much of the world was in a state of collapse after World War II.

But where is globalization now that we need it? Did it turn out that we really weren't all living together on a single, shrinking planet? Were the globalists of that moment inhabiting another planet entirely in another solar system? Or could it be that globalization is still the ruling paradigm here, but that what's globalizing isn't (or isn't just) Pizza Huts, iMacs, and Lexuses, but pressure points for the fracturing of our world?

The globalization of misery doesn't have the cachet of the globalization of plenty. It doesn't make for the same uplifting reading, nor does skyrocketing global economic inequality seem quite as thrilling as a leveling playing field (unless, of course, you happen to be a billionaire). And thanks significantly to the military efforts of the last superpower standing, the disintegration of significant regions of the planet doesn't quite add up to what the globalists had in mind for the twenty-first century. Failed states, spreading terror movements, all too many Mosuls, and the conditions for so much more of the same weren't what globalization was supposed to be all about.

Perhaps, however, it's time to begin reminding ourselves that we're still on a globalizing planet, even if one experiencing pressures of an unexpected sort, including from the disastrous never-ending American war on terror. It's so much more convenient, of course, to throw the idea of globalization overboard and imagine that Mosul is thousands of miles away in a universe that bears next to no relation to our own.

What It Really Means
to Be on a "Flattening" Planet

It's true that in France extremist presidential candidate Marine Le Pen was defeated by a young, little-known former investment banker and government minister, Emmanuel Macron, and the European Union was preserved. As with an earlier election in Holland in which a similar right-wing candidate lost, this election victory is being presented as potentially the high-water mark of what's now commonly called "populism" in Europe (or the Brexit-style fragmentation of that continent). But I'd take such reassurances with a grain of salt, given the pressures likely to come. After all, in both Holland and France, two extreme nationalist parties garnered record votes based on anti-Islamic, anti-refugee sentiment, and will, after the coming parliamentary elections in France, both be represented, again in record numbers, in their legislatures.

The rise of such "populism" is already a global trend. So just imagine the situation four or potentially even eight years from now after Donald Trump's generals, already in the saddle, do their damnedest in the Greater Middle East and Africa. There's no reason to believe that, under their direction, the smashing of key regions of the planet won't continue. There's no reason to doubt that, in an expanding world of Mosuls, "victories" won't produce a planet of greater ethnic savagery, religious extremism, military destruction, and chaos. This, in turn, ensures a further spread of terror groups and an even more staggering displacement of peoples. (It's worth noting, for instance, that since the death of Osama bin Laden at the hands of US special operations forces, al-Qaeda has grown, not shrunk, gaining yet more traction across the Greater Middle East.) So far, America's permanent war on terror has helped produce a planet of fear and ever-more terror. What else would you imagine could arise from the rubble of so many Mosuls?

If you don't think that this is an ever-more connected planet still being "flattened" (even if in quite a different way than expected), and that sooner or later the destruction of Mosul will reverberate in our world, too, then you don't get our world. It's obvious, for instance, that future Mosuls will only produce more refugees. Destroy enough

Mosuls and, even in the heartland of the planet's sole superpower, the fears of those who already feel they've been left in a ditch will only rise—and be fed further by demagogues ready to use that global flow of refugees for their own purposes.

Given the transformations of recent years, just think what it will mean to uproot ever vaster populations, to set the desperate, the angry, the hurt, and the vengeful—millions of adults and children whose lives have been devastated or destroyed—in motion. Imagine, for instance, what those pressures will mean when it comes to Europe and its future politics.

Think about what's to come on this small planet of ours—and that's without even mentioning the force that has yet to fully reveal itself, in all its fragmenting and globalizing and leveling power. We now call this force, mildly enough, "climate change" or "global warming." Just wait until, in the decades to come, rising sea levels and extreme weather events put human beings in motion in startling ways—particularly given that the planet's sole superpower is now run by men in violent denial of the very existence of such a force or the human sources of its power.

You want a shrinking planet? You want terror? You want globalization? Think about that. And do you wonder why, these days, I have Mosul on my mind?

Osama Bin Laden's America

Honestly, if there's an afterlife, then the soul of Osama bin Laden, whose body was consigned to the waves by the US Navy back in 2011, must be swimming happily with the dolphins and sharks. At the cost of the sort of a mere $400,000 to $500,000, bin Laden managed to launch the American war on terror. He did so with little but a clever game plan, a few fanatical followers, and a remarkably intuitive sense of how this country works.

He had those nineteen mostly Saudi hijackers, a scattering of supporters elsewhere in the world, and the "training camps" in Afghanistan, but his was a ragged and understaffed movement. And keep in mind that his sworn enemy was the country that then prided itself on being the winner of the imperial sweepstakes that had gone on for five centuries until, in 1991, the Soviet Union imploded.

His challenge was: with such limited resources, what kind of self-destructive behavior could he goad a triumphalist Washington into? The key would be what might be called apocalyptic humiliation.

Looking back, it's extraordinary how September 11, 2001, would set the pattern for everything that followed. Each further goading act, from Afghanistan to Libya, San Bernardino to Manhattan, Iraq to Niger, each further humiliation would trigger yet more of the same behavior in Washington. After all, so many people and institutions came to have a vested interest in Osama bin Laden's version of our world.

Apocalyptic Humiliation

Grim as the 9/11 attacks were, they would be but the start of bin Laden's "success," which has, in truth, never ended. That 9/11 had "changed everything"—the phrase of that moment—proved far more devastatingly accurate than we Americans imagined at the time.

After all, Osama bin Laden managed to involve the United States in sixteen years of fruitless wars with no end in sight. At the same time, he helped turn twenty-first-century Washington into a war machine of the first order that ate the rest of the American government for lunch. He gave the national security state the means—the excuse, if you will—to rise to a kind of power, prominence, and funding that might otherwise have been inconceivable. In the process—undoubtedly fulfilling his wildest dreams—he helped speed up the decline of the very country that, since the Cold War ended, had been plugging itself as the greatest ever.

In other words, bin Laden may truly be the (malign) genius of our age. He created a terrorist version of call-and-response that still rules Donald Trump's Washington, in which the rubblized generals of America's rubblized wars on an increasingly rubblized planet now reign supreme. In other words, The Donald, James "Mad Dog" Mattis, John Kelly, and H. R. McMaster were Osama bin Laden's grim gift to the rest of us. Thanks to him, literally trillions of taxpayer dollars would go down the tubes in remarkably pointless wars followed by "reconstruction" scams abroad that threaten to feed on each other to something like the end of (American) time.

Of course, he had a little luck in the process. As a start, no one, not even the 9/11 plotters, could have imagined that those towers in Manhattan would collapse before the already omnipresent cameras of the age in a way that would create such classically apocalyptic imagery. As scholar Paul Boyer once argued, in the wake of Hiroshima and Nagasaki, Americans never stopped dreaming of a nuclear attack on this country. Our pop culture was filled with such nightmares. On that September day, many Americans suddenly felt as if something like it had finally occurred. It wasn't happenstance that, within twenty-four hours, the area of downtown Manhattan where the shards of those towers lay would be dubbed "Ground Zero," a term previously reserved for the spot where a nuclear explosion had taken place, or that Tom Brokaw, anchoring NBC's nonstop news coverage, would claim that it was "like a nuclear winter in lower Manhattan."

The sense of having been subjected to a sneak attack on an apocalyptic scale—hence the "new Pearl Harbor" and "Day of Infamy" headlines—proved overwhelming as the scenes of those towers falling in a near mushroom cloud of smoke and ash were endlessly replayed. Of course, no such apocalyptic attack had occurred. The weapons at hand weren't even bombs or missiles, but our own airplanes filled with passengers. And yes, it was a horror, but not the horror Americans generally took it for. And yet, sixteen years later, it's still impossible to put 9/11 in any kind of reasonable context or perspective in this country, even after we've helped to rubblize major cities across the Middle East and so aided in creating landscapes far more post-apocalyptic than Ground Zero ever was.

On the other hand, imagine where we'd be if Osama bin Laden had had just a little more luck that day; imagine if the fourth hijacked plane, the one that crashed in a field in Pennsylvania, had actually reached its target in Washington and wiped out, say, the White House.

Bin Laden certainly chose his symbols of American power well— financial (the World Trade Center), military (the Pentagon), and political (some target in Washington)—in order to make the government and people of the self-proclaimed most exceptional nation on Earth feel the deepest possible sense of humiliation. Bin Laden could hardly have hit a more American nerve or created a stronger sense that the country that felt it had everything was now left with nothing at all.

That it wasn't true—not faintly—didn't matter. And add in one more bit of bin Laden good luck. The administration in the White House at that moment had its own overblown dreams of how our world should work. As they emerged from the shock of those attacks, which sent Vice President Dick Cheney into a Cold War–era underground nuclear bunker, they began to dream of their global moment. Like Defense Secretary Donald Rumsfeld in the partially destroyed Pentagon, they instantly started thinking about taking out Iraq's autocratic ruler Saddam Hussein and launching a project to create a Middle East and then a planet over which the United States alone would have dominion forever.

As befit those Pearl Harbor headlines, on the night of September 11, the president was already speaking of "the war against terrorism." Within a day, he had called it "the first war of the twenty-first century" and soon, because al-Qaeda was such a pathetically inadequate target, had added, "Our war on terror begins with al-Qaeda, but it does not end there."

It couldn't have been stranger. The United States was "at war," but not with a great power or even one of the regional "rogue states" that had been the focus of American military thinking in the 1990s. We were at war with a phenomenon—"terrorism"—on a global scale. As Rumsfeld would say only five days after 9/11, the new war on terror would be "a large multi-headed effort that probably spans sixty countries, including the United States." In the phrase of that moment, we were going to "drain the swamp" globally.

Even setting aside that terrorism then had no real armies, no real territory, essentially nothing, this plan for global warfare couldn't have been more wildly out of proportion to what had actually happened or to the outfit that had caused it to happen. But anyone who suggested as much (or an alternative as simple and unimpressive as a "police action" against bin Laden and crew) was promptly laughed out of the room or abused into silence. And so a call-and-response pattern that fit bin Laden's wildest dreams would be established in which, whatever they did, the United States would always respond by militarily upping the ante.

In this way, Washington promptly found itself plunged into a Global War on Terror that was essentially a figment of its own imagination. The Bush administration, not Osama bin Laden, then proceeded to turn it into a reality, starting with the invasions and occupations of Afghanistan and Iraq. Meanwhile, from the passage of the Patriot Act to the establishment of the Department of Homeland Security, a newly national-securitized Washington would be built up on a previously unheard of scale.

In other words, we were already entering Osama bin Laden's America.

The War Lovers

In this way, long before Donald Trump and Rex Tillerson began downsizing the State Department, George W. Bush and his top officials committed themselves to the US military as the option of choice for what had previously been called "foreign policy." They had little doubt that they possessed a force beyond compare with the kind of power and technological resources guaranteed to sweep away everything before it. What, then, could possibly stop it from spearheading the establishment of a *Pax Americana* in the Greater Middle East and then globally?

As it happened, the key officials of the Bush administration had absorbed nothing of the twentieth-century history of insurrection, rebellion, and resistance in the former colonial world. If they had, none of what followed would have surprised them in the least.

And so, the wars would spread, states would begin to crumble, terror movements would multiply, and each little shiver of fear, each set of American deaths, whether by such movements or "lone wolves" in the United States and Europe, would call up just one response from the government: more of the same.

Think of this as Osama bin Laden's dream world.

I've been writing about this at *TomDispatch* year after year for a decade and a half now and nothing ever changes. Not really. It's all so sadly predictable as, years after bin Laden was consigned to his watery grave, Washington continues essentially to do his bidding in a remarkably brainless fashion.

Think of it as a kind of feedback loop in which the interests of a domestic security and surveillance state, built to monumental proportions against a relatively minor fear (of terrorism), and a military eternally funded to the heavens on a remarkably bipartisan basis for its never-ending war on terror ensure that nothing ever truly changes. In twenty-first-century Washington, failure is the new success and repetition is the rule of the day, week, month, and year.

Take, for example, the events in Niger in early October 2017. Consider the pattern of call-and-response there. Almost no Americans (and it turned out, next to no senators) even knew that the United States had something like nine hundred troops deployed permanently to that West African country and two drone bases there (though it was no secret). Then, on October 4, the first reports of the deaths of four American soldiers and the wounding of two others in a Green Beret unit on a "routine training mission" in the lawless Niger-Mali border area came out. The ambush, it seemed, had been set by an ISIS affiliate.

It was, in fact, such an obscure and distant event that, for almost two weeks, there was little reaction in Congress or a media uproar of any sort. That ended, however, when President Trump, in response to questions about those dead soldiers, attacked Barack Obama and George W. Bush for not calling the parents of the American fallen (they had) and then got into a dispute with the widow of one of the Niger dead (as well as a Democratic congresswoman) over his condolence call to her. The head of the Joint Chiefs was soon forced to hold a news conference; former four-star Marine general and White House Chief of Staff John Kelly, whose son had died in Afghanistan, felt called upon to go to the mat for his boss, falsely accuse that congresswoman, and essentially claim that the military was now an elite caste in this country. This certainly reflected the new highly militarized sense of power and worth that lay at the heart of bin Laden's Washington.

It was only then that the event in distant Niger became another terrorist humiliation of the first order. Senators were suddenly outraged. Senator John McCain (one of the more warlike members of that body, famous in 2007 for jokingly singing, to the tune of an old Beach Boys song, "Bomb, bomb, bomb Iran") threatened to subpoena the administration for more Niger information. Meanwhile his friend Senator Lindsey Graham, another war hawk of the first order, issued a classic warning of this era: "We don't want the next 9/11 to come from Niger!"

And suddenly US Africa Command was highlighting its desire for more money from Congress, the military was moving to arm its Reaper drones in Niger with Hellfire missiles for future counterterrorism operations, and Secretary of Defense Mattis was assuring senators privately that the military would "expand" its "counterterrorism focus" in Africa. The military began to prepare to deploy Hellfire missile–armed Reaper drones to Niger. "The war is morphing," Graham insisted. "You're going to see more actions in Africa, not less; you're going to see more aggression by the United States toward our enemies, not less; you're going to have decisions being made not in the White House but out in the field."

Rumors were soon floating around that, as the *Washington Post* reported, the administration might "loosen restrictions on the US military's ability to use lethal force in Niger" (as it already has done in the Trump era in places like Syria and Yemen). And so it expectedly went, as events in Niger proceeded from utter obscurity to the near-apocalyptic, while—despite the strangeness of the Trumpian moment—the responses came in exactly as anyone reviewing the last sixteen years might have imagined they would.

All of this will predictably make things in central Africa worse, not better, leading to . . . well, more than a decade and a half after 9/11, you know just as well as I do where it's leading. And there are remarkably few brakes on the situation, especially with three generals of our losing wars ruling the roost in Washington and Donald Trump now lashed to the mast of his chief of staff.

Welcome to Osama bin Laden's America.

EIGHT

A Nation Unmade by War

In March 2017, I visited two museum exhibitions that captured something of a lost American world and seemed eerily relevant in the age
of Trump. The first, "Hippie Modernism," an exploration of the coun-
terculture of the 1960s and 1970s (heavy on psychedelic posters), was
appropriately enough at the Berkeley Art Museum. To my surprise,
it also included a few artifacts from a movement crucial to my own
not-especially-countercultural version of those years: the vast antiwar
protests that took to the streets in the mid-1960s, shook the country,
and never really went away until the last American combat troops
were finally withdrawn from Vietnam in 1973. Included was a poster
of the American flag, upside down, its stripes redrawn as red rifles, its
stars as blue fighter planes, and another showing an American soldier,
a rifle casually slung over his shoulder. Its caption still seems relevant
as our never-ending wars continue to head for "the homeland."

"Violence abroad," it read, "breeds violence at home." Amen, brother.

The next day, I went to a small Rosie the Riveter Memorial museum-
cum-visitor's center in a national park in Richmond, California, on the
shores of San Francisco Bay. There, during World War II, workers at a
giant Ford plant assembled tanks, while Henry Kaiser's nearby shipyard
complex was, at one point, launching a Liberty or Victory ship every single

day. Let me repeat that: on average, one ship *a day*. Almost three-quarters of a century later, that rate remains mindboggling. In fact, those yards, as I learned from a documentary at the visitor's center, set a record by constructing a single cargo ship, stem to stern, in just under five days.

And what made such records and that kind of 24/7 productiveness possible in wartime America? All of it happened largely because the gates to the American workforce were suddenly thrown open not just to Rosie, the famed riveter, and so many other women whose opportunities had previously been limited largely to gender-stereotyped jobs, but to African Americans, Chinese Americans, the aged, the disabled, just about everyone in town (except incarcerated Japanese Americans) who had previously been left out or sold short, a sort of cross-section of a country that wouldn't rub elbows again for decades.

Similarly, the vast antiwar movement of the 1960s and early 1970s was filled with an unexpected cross-section of the country, including middle-class students and largely working-class vets directly off the battlefields of Southeast Asia. Both the workforce of those World War II years and the protest movement of their children were, in their own fashion, citizen wonders of their American moments. They were artifacts of a country in which the public was still believed to play a crucial role and in which government of the people, by the people, and for the people didn't yet sound like a late-night laugh line. Having seen in those museum exhibitions traces of two surges of civic duty—if you don't mind my repurposing the word "surge," now used only for military operations leading nowhere—I suddenly realized that my family (like so many other American families) had been deeply affected by each of those mobilizing moments, one in support of a war and the other in opposition to it.

My father joined the US Army Air Corps immediately after the Japanese attack on Pearl Harbor. He became operations officer for the First Air Commandos in Burma. My mother joined the mobilization back home, becoming chair of the Artist's Committee of the American Theatre Wing, which, among other things, planned entertainment for servicemen and women. In every sense, theirs was a war of citizens' mobilization—from those rivets pounded in by Rosie to the backyard "victory gardens" (more than twenty million of them) that sprang up nationwide and played a significant role in feeding the country in a time of global crisis. And then there were the war bond drives, for one of which my mother, described in an ad as a "well-known caricaturist of stage and screen stars," agreed to do "a caricature of those who purchase a $500 war bond or more."

World War II was distinctly a citizen's war. I was born in 1944 just as it was reaching its climax. My own version of such a mobilization, two decades later, took me by surprise. In my youth, I had dreamed of serving my country by becoming a State Department official and representing it abroad. In a land that still had a citizen's army and a draft, it never crossed my mind that I wouldn't also be in the military at some point, doing my duty. That my "duty" in those years would instead turn out to involve joining in a mobilization against war was unexpected. But that an American citizen should care about the wars that his (or her) country fought and why it fought them was second nature. Those wars—both against fascism globally and against rebellious peasants across much of Southeast Asia—were distinctly American projects. That meant they were our responsibility.

If my country fought the war from hell in a distant land, killing peasants by the endless thousands, it seemed only natural, a duty in fact, to react to it as so many Americans drafted into that military did—even wearing peace symbols into battle, creating antiwar newspapers on their military bases, and essentially going into opposition while still in that citizen's army. The horror of that war mobilized me, too, just not from within the military itself. And yet I can still remember that when I marched on Washington, along with hundreds of thousands of other protesters, it never occurred to me—not even when Richard Nixon was in the White House—that an American president wouldn't have to listen to the voices of a mobilized citizenry.

Each of those mobilizing moments, in its own curious fashion, proved to be a distinctly American tale of triumph: the victory of World War II that left fascism in its German, Italian, and Japanese forms in literal ruins, while turning the United States into a global superpower; and the defeat in Vietnam, which checked that superpower's capacity to destroy, thanks at least in part to the actions of both a citizen's army in revolt and an army of citizens.

The Teflon Objects of Our American World

Since then, in every sense, victory has gone missing in action and so, for decades (with a single brief moment of respite), has the very idea that Americans have a duty of any sort when it comes to the wars their country chooses to fight. In our era, war, like the Pentagon budget and the growing powers of the national security state, has been inoculated against the virus of citizen involvement, and so against any significant form of criticism or resistance. It's a process worth contemplating since it reminds us that we're truly in a new American age, whether of the plutocrats, by the plutocrats, and for the plutocrats or of the generals, by the generals, and for the generals—but most distinctly not of the people, by the people, and for the people.

After all, for more than sixteen years, the US military has been fighting essentially failed or failing wars—conflicts that only seem to spread the phenomenon (terrorism) they're supposed to eradicate—in Afghanistan, Iraq, more recently Syria, intermittently Yemen, and elsewhere across the Greater Middle East and parts of Africa. Recently, civilians in those distant lands have been dying in rising numbers (to remarkably little attention in the United States). Meanwhile, Donald Trump's generals have been quietly escalating those wars. Hundreds, possibly thousands, more American soldiers and special ops forces are being sent into Syria, Iraq, and neighboring Kuwait (about which the Pentagon will no longer provide even inaccurate numbers); US air strikes have been on the rise throughout the region; the American commander in Afghanistan is calling for reinforcements; drone strikes recently set a new record for intensity in Yemen; Somalia may be the next target of mission creep and escalation; and it looks as if Iran is now in Washington's sniper scopes.

It's worth noting here that even with a significant set of anti-Trump groups taking to the streets in protest, none are focused on America's wars.

Many of these developments were reasonably predictable once Donald Trump—a man unconcerned with the details of anything from healthcare to bombing campaigns—appointed generals already deeply implicated in America's disastrous wars to plan and oversee his version of them, as well as to oversee foreign policy generally. (Rex Tillerson's State Department has, by now, been relegated to near nonentity-hood.) In response, many in the media and elsewhere began treating those generals as if they were the only "adults" in the Trumpian room. If so, they are distinctly deluded ones, otherwise why would they be ramping up their wars in a fashion familiar to anyone who's been paying attention for the last decade and a half, clearly resorting to more of what hasn't worked in all these years? We already know how this story ends, having had so many grim lessons on the subject. The question is: Why don't the generals?

Another question that should (but doesn't) come to mind in twenty-first-century America is why does a war effort that has already cost taxpayers trillions of dollars not involve the slightest mobilization of the American people? No war taxes, war bonds, war drives, victory gardens, sacrifice of any sort, or for that matter even serious criticism, protest, or resistance? As has been true since Vietnam, war and American national security are thought to be best left to the pros, even if those pros have proven a distinctly amateurish lot.

Indeed, with an opposition movement gearing up on domestic issues, will our wars, the military, and the national security state continue to be the Teflon objects of our American world? Why, with the sole exception of President Trump (and in his case only when it comes to the way the country's intelligence agencies have dealt with him) is no one—other than small groups of antiwar vets and a tiny number of similarly determined activists—going after the national security state, even as its wars threaten to create a vast arc of failed states and a hell of terror movements and unmoored populations?

The Age of Demobilization

In the case of America's wars, there's a history that helps explain how we ended up in such a situation. It would undoubtedly begin with an American high command facing a military in near revolt in the later Vietnam years and agreeing, after much hesitation, that what was needed was an "all-volunteer" force (which, to them, meant a no-protest one).

In 1973, President Nixon obliged and ended the draft, the first step in bringing a rebellious citizen's army and a rebellious populace back under control. In the decades to come, the military would be transformed—though few here would say such a thing—into something closer to an American foreign legion. In addition, in the post–9/11 years, that all-volunteer force came to shelter within it a second, far more secretive military, seventy thousand strong: the US Special Operations Command. Members of that elite crew, which might be thought of as the president's private army, are now regularly dispatched around the globe to train literal foreign legions and to commit deeds that are, at best, only half known to the American people.

In these years, Americans have largely been convinced that secrecy is the single most crucial factor in national security; that what we do know will hurt us; and that ignorance of the workings of our own government, now enswathed in a penumbra of secrecy, will help keep us safe from "terror." In other words, knowledge is danger and ignorance, safety. However Orwellian that may sound, it has become the norm of twenty-first-century America.

That the government must have the power to surveil us is by now a given. That our government's actions must also be kept secret from us is its corollary. And the combination has proven an effective formula for the kind of demobilization that has come to define this era, even if it fits poorly with any normal definition of how a democracy should function or with the now exceedingly old-fashioned belief that an informed public (as opposed to an uninformed or even misinformed one) is crucial to the workings of such a government.

In addition, as they launched their Global War on Terror after 9/11, top Bush administration officials remained haunted by memories of the anti–Vietnam War mobilization. They were eager for wars in which there would be no prying journalists, no ugly body counts, and no body bags heading home to protesting citizens. In their minds, there were to be only two roles available for the American public. The first was, in President George W. Bush's classic formulation, to "go down to Disney World in Florida, take your families, and enjoy life the way we want it to be enjoyed"—in other words, go shopping. The second was to eternally thank and praise America's "warriors" for their deeds and efforts. Their wars for better or worse (and it would invariably turn out to be for worse) were intended to be people-less ones in distant lands that would in no way disturb American life—another fantasy of our age.

Coverage of the resulting wars would be carefully controlled; journalists "embedded" in the military; (American) casualties kept as low as possible; and warfare itself made secretive, "smart," and increasingly robotic (think: drones) with death a one-way street for the enemy. American-style war was, in short, to become unimaginably antiseptic and distant (if, that is, you were living thousands of miles away and busy shopping your heart out). In addition, the memory of the attacks of 9/11 helped sanitize whatever the United States did thereafter.

The result at home would be an age of demobilization. The single exception—and it's one that historians will perhaps someday puzzle over—being the few months leading up to the Bush administration's invasion of Iraq in which hundreds of thousands of Americans (and millions globally) suddenly took to the streets in repeated protests. That, however, largely ended with the actual invasion and in the face of a government determined not to listen.

It remains to be seen whether, in Donald Trump's America, with that sense of demobilization fading, America's wars and military-first policies will once again become the targets of a mobilizing public. Or will Trump and his Teflon generals have a free hand to do as they want abroad, no matter what happens at home?

In many ways, from its founding the United States has been a nation made by wars. The question in this century is: Will its citizenry and its form of government be unmade by them?

"Tell Me How This Ends?" David Petraeus Finally Answers His Own Question

It took fourteen years, but now we have an answer.

It was March 2003, the invasion of Iraq was underway, and Major General David Petraeus was in command of the 101st Airborne Division heading for the Iraqi capital, Baghdad. Rick Atkinson, *Washington Post* journalist and military historian, was accompanying him.

Six days into a lightning campaign, his division suddenly found itself stopped thirty miles southwest of the city of Najaf by terrible weather, including a blinding dust storm, and the unexpectedly "fanatical" attacks of Iraqi irregulars. At that moment, Atkinson reported:

> [Petraeus] hooked his thumbs into his flak vest and adjusted the weight on his shoulders. "Tell me how this ends," he said. "Eight years and eight divisions?" The allusion was to advice supposedly given the White House in the early 1950s by a senior Army strategist upon being asked what it would take to prop up French forces in South Vietnam. Petraeus's grin suggested the comment was more droll quip than historical assertion.

Certainly, Petraeus knew his history when it came to American interventions in distant lands. He had entered West Point just as the American war in Vietnam was beginning to wind down and did his doctoral dissertation at Princeton in 1987 on that conflict ("The American Military and the Lessons of Vietnam: A Study of Military Influence and the Use of Force in the Post-Vietnam Era"). In it, he wrote:

> Vietnam cost the military dearly. It left America's military leaders confounded, dismayed, and discouraged. Even worse, it devastated the armed forces, robbing them of dignity, money, and qualified people for a decade. Vietnam was an extremely painful reminder that when it comes to intervention, time and patience are not American virtues in abundant supply.

So, no wonder he was well acquainted with that 1954 exchange between President Dwight D. Eisenhower and former Korean War commander General Matthew Ridgeway about the French war in Vietnam. Perhaps, the "droll quip" aspect of his comment lay in his knowledge of just how badly Ridgeway underestimated both the years and the troop numbers that the American war there would eat up before it, too, ended in disaster and in a military as riddled with protest and as close to collapse as was imaginable for an American force of our era.

In his thesis, Petraeus called for the military high command to be granted a far freer hand in whatever interventions the future held. In that sense, in 1987, he was already mainlining into a twenty-first-century world in which the US military continues to get everything it wants (and more) as it fights its wars without having to deal with either an obstreperous citizen army or too many politicians trying to impose their will on its actions.

And by the way, though his Najaf comments have regularly been cited as if they were *sui generis*, as the Ridgeway reference indicates, Petraeus was hardly the first American military commander or political figure to appropriate Joan of Arc's question in Bernard Shaw's play *Saint Joan*: "How long, oh Lord, how long?"

As Pulitzer Prize–winning journalist David Halberstam recounted in his history of the Vietnam years, *The Best and the Brightest*, President Lyndon Johnson turned to Joint Chiefs Chairman General Earle Wheeler in a June 1965 meeting and asked of the war in Vietnam, "What do you think it will take to do the job?" Wheeler's answer echoed Ridgeway's eleven years earlier, though in the escalatory mode that was typical of Vietnam:

> It all depends on what your definition of the job is, Mr. President. If you intend to drive the last Vietcong out of Vietnam it will take seven hundred, eight hundred thousand, a million men and about seven years. But if your definition of the job is to prevent the Communists from taking over the country, that is, stopping them from doing it, then you're talking about different gradations and different levels. So tell us what the job is and we'll answer it.

A Generational Approach to America's Wars

Not so long after that moment on the outskirts of Najaf, the 101st Airborne made its way to Baghdad just as the burning and looting began, and that would only be the prologue to David Petraeus's war, to his version of eight years and eight divisions. When an insurgency (actually several) broke out in Iraq, he would be dispatched to the northern city of Mosul. There, he would first experiment with bringing back from the Vietnam experience the very strategy the US military had hoped to be rid of forever: "counterinsurgency," or the winning of what in that war had regularly been called "hearts and minds." In

2004, *Newsweek* was already hailing him on its cover with the dramatic question: "Can This Man Save Iraq?" (Four months after Petraeus ended his stint in that city, the police chief he had trained there went over to the insurgents and it became a stronghold for them.)

By the time the occupation of Iraq turned into a full-scale disaster, he was back at Fort Leavenworth running the US Army's Combined Arms Center. During that period, he and another officer, Marine Lieutenant General James Mattis—does that name ring any bells?—joined forces to oversee the development and publication of *Field Service Manual 3-24: Counterinsurgency Operations*. It would be the first official counterinsurgency (COIN) how-to book the military had produced since the Vietnam years. In the process, Petraeus became "the world's leading expert in counterinsurgency warfare." He would famously return to Iraq in 2007, that manual in hand, with five brigades, or twenty thousand US troops, for what would become known as "the surge," or "the new way forward," an attempt to bail the Bush administration out of its disastrous occupation of the country. His counterinsurgency operations would, like the initial invasion, be hailed by experts and pundits in Washington (including Petraeus himself) as a marvel and a success of the first order, as a true turning point in Iraq and in the war on terror.

A decade after that "new way forward," with America's third Iraq War ongoing, you could be excused for viewing the "successes" of that surge somewhat differently.

In the process, Petraeus (or "King David," as he was supposedly nicknamed by Iraqis during his stint in Mosul) became America's most celebrated, endlessly featured general, and went on in 2008 to head US Central Command (overseeing America's wars in both Afghanistan and Iraq). In 2010, he became the US Afghan commander, largely so that he could perform the counterinsurgency miracles in Afghanistan he had supposedly performed in Iraq. In 2011, he became Barack Obama's CIA director only to crash and burn a year later in a scandal over a lover-cum-biographer and the misuse of classified documents, after which he morphed into a go-to expert on our wars and a partner at KKR, a global investment firm. In other words, as with the three generals of the surge generation now ascendant in Washington, including Petraeus's former COIN pal James Mattis (who also once headed the US Central Command), he presided over this country's failing wars in the Greater Middle East.

And only recently, fourteen years after he and Atkinson were briefly trapped outside Najaf, in his current role as a pundit and prognosticator on his former wars, he finally answered—and not as a quip either—the question that plagued him then. Though his comments were certainly covered in the news (as anything he says is), in a sense no one noticed. Asked by Judy Woodruff of the PBS *NewsHour* whether, in Donald Trump's America, it was "smart" to once again send more US troops surging into Afghanistan, Petraeus called the Pentagon's decision "heartening," even as he warned that it wasn't a war that would end any time soon. After so many years of involvement, experience, thought, and observation, from a studio without a grain of sand, no less a dust storm in sight, he offered this observation:

> But this is a generational struggle. This is not something that is going to be won in a few years. We're not going to take a hill, plant a flag, [and] go home to a victory parade. And we need to be there for the long haul, but in a way that is, again, sustainable. We have been in Korea for sixty-five-plus years because there is an important national interest for that. We were in Europe for a very long period of time, still there, of course, and actually with a renewed emphasis now, given Russia's aggressive actions. And I think that's the way we need to approach this.

In proposing such a "generational struggle" to be handed on to our children, if not grandchildren, Petraeus is in good company. In recent times, the Pentagon high command, too, has adopted a "generational approach" to Afghanistan and assumedly our other wars across the Greater Middle East and Africa. Similarly, the scholars of the Brookings Institution have urged on Washington's policymakers what they call "an enduring partnership" in Afghanistan: "The U.S.-Afghan partnership should be recognized as generational in duration, given the nature of the threat and the likely longevity of its future manifestations."

Even if, under further questioning by Woodruff, Petraeus wouldn't quite cop to a sixty-year Afghan war (that is, to a war lasting at least until 2061), his long-delayed answer to his own question of the 2003 invasion moment was now definitive. Such American wars won't end. Not now. Maybe not ever. And in a way, you can't be much blunter or grimmer than that in your assessment of the "successes" of the war on terror.

A Military Success Story of the Strangest Sort

Until James "Mad Dog" Mattis hit Washington in 2017, no American general of our era was ever written about as much as, or in a more celebratory fashion than, David Petraeus. Adulatory (if not fawning) profiles of him are legion. Even today, in the wake of barely avoided felony and other charges (for, among other things, lying to the FBI)—he pleaded guilty to a misdemeanor for the mishandling of classified documents and was sentenced to two years of probation and a fine—he may still be this country's most celebrated general.

But why exactly such celebration? The answer would have to be that he continues to be considered a must-quote expert only because in Washington this country's war on terror and the generalship that's accompanied it are now beyond serious analysis or reconsideration. Sixteen years after the invasion of Afghanistan, as America's wars continue to spread across the Greater Middle East and Africa, its generals are now treated like the only "adults in the room" in our nation's capital, like, in short, American winners.

And yet, consider events in the central African country of Niger, which already has an operating US drone base, another under construction, and about eight hundred American troops quietly but permanently stationed there. It's also a country that not an American in a million would have been able to locate on a map, not until four Green Berets were killed and two others wounded during a "routine training mission" there on October 4, 2017. Patrolling with Nigerien troops, they were ambushed by Islamic militants—whether from al-Qaeda in the Islamic Maghreb or a new branch of ISIS remains unclear. That officially makes Niger at least the eighth country, including Pakistan, Afghanistan, Iraq, Yemen, Syria, Somalia, and Libya, to be absorbed into

Washington's war on terror and, in case you hadn't noticed, in none of them has that war yet ended and in none have US forces triumphed.

Even so, you could comb the recent mainstream coverage of the events in Niger without finding any indication that those deaths represented a modest new escalation in the never-ending, ever-spreading war on terror.

As was inevitable, in Iraq and Syria, Abu Bakr al-Baghdadi's Islamic "caliphate" is finally collapsing. In what are now the ravaged ruins of Syria and Iraq, however, such "victories" will inevitably prove as hollow as were the "successful" invasions of Afghanistan and Iraq or the "successful" overthrow of Libyan autocrat Muammar Gaddafi. Meanwhile, the Islamic State may have spread its brand to Niger, another country with US forces in it. Nevertheless, across a vast swath of the planet, the wars of David Petraeus, James Mattis, and the other generals of this era simply go on and on.

Worse yet, it's a situation that can't be seriously discussed in this country because, if it were, opposition to those wars might rise and alternatives to the by-now–brain-dead decisions of those generals, including newly heightened air wars and the latest mini-surge in Afghanistan, might become part of an actual national debate.

So, think of this as a military success story of the strangest sort—success that can be traced directly back to a single decision, now decades old, made by a long-discredited American president, Richard Nixon. Without returning to that decision, there is simply no way to understand America's twenty-first-century wars. In its own way, it would prove an act of genius (if, at least, you wanted to fight never-ending wars until the end of time).

In any case, credit, when owed, must be given. Facing an antiwar movement that wouldn't go away and that, by the early 1970s, included significant numbers of both active-duty servicemen and Vietnam veterans, the president and his secretary of defense, Melvin Laird, decided to try to cut into its strength by eliminating the draft. Nixon suspected that young men not endangered by the possibility of being sent into the Vietnam War might be far less eager to demonstrate against it. The military high command was uncertain about such a move. They worried, with reason, that in the wake of Vietnam it would be hard to recruit for an all-volunteer military. Who in the world, they wondered, would want to be part of such a discredited force? That was, of course, a version of Nixon's thinking turned upside down, but the president moved ahead anyway and, on January 27, 1973, conscription was ended. There would be no more draft calls and the citizen's army, the one that had fought World War II to victory and had raised such a ruckus about the grim and distasteful war in Vietnam, would be no more.

In that single stroke, before he himself fell prey to the Watergate scandal and resigned his presidency, Nixon functionally created a legacy for the ages, paving the way for the American military to fight its wars "generationally" and continue losing them until hell froze over, with the guarantee that no one in this country would seem to care a whit. Or put another way, can you truly imagine such silence in "the homeland" if an American draft were continually filling the ranks of a citizen's army to fight a sixteen-year-old war on terror, still spreading, and now considered "generational"? I doubt it.

So as American air power in places like Yemen, Somalia, and Afghanistan is ramped up yet again, as the latest mini-surge of troops arrives in Afghanistan, as Niger enters the war, it's time to put generals David Petraeus, James Mattis, H. R. McMaster, and John Kelly in context. It's time to call them what they truly are: Nixon's children.

POSTSCRIPT

Fiddling through the Smoke in 2025

It's January 2025, and within days of entering the Oval Office, a new president already faces his first full-scale crisis abroad. Twenty-four years after it began, the war on terror, from the Philippines to Nigeria, rages on. In 2024 alone, the United States launched repeated air strikes on sixteen nations (or, in a number of cases, former nations), including the Philippines, Myanmar, Pakistan, Afghanistan, Yemen, the former Republic of Iraq, the former Syrian Arab Republic, Kurdistan, Turkey, Saudi Arabia, Egypt, Tunisia, Libya, Mali, Niger, and Nigeria.

In the weeks before his inauguration, a series of events roiled the Greater Middle East and Africa. Drone strikes and raids by US special operations forces in Saudi Arabia against both Shiite rebels and militants from the Global Islamic State killed scores of civilians, including children. They left that increasingly destabilized kingdom in an uproar, intensified the unpopularity of its young king, and led to the withdrawal of the Saudi ambassador from Washington. In Mali, three Islamic militants from the Front Azawad, which now controls the upper third of the country, dressed in police uniforms and riding on motorcycles, gained entry to a recently established joint US-French military base and blew themselves up, killing six American Green Berets, three American contractors, and two French soldiers, while wounding several members of Mali's presidential guard. In

Iraq, as 2024 ended, the city of Tal Afar—already liberated twice since the 2003 invasion of that country, first by American troops in 2005 and then by American-backed Iraqi troops in 2017—fell to the Sunni militants of the Global Islamic State. Though now besieged by the forces of the Republic of Southern Iraq backed by the US Air Force, it remains in their hands.

The crisis of the moment, however, is in Afghanistan where the war on terror first began. There, the Taliban, the Global Islamic State (or GIS, which emerged from the Islamic State, or ISIS, in 2019), and al-Qaeda in Afghanistan (or AQIA, which split from the original al-Qaeda in 2021) control an increasing number of provincial capitals, all now in ruins. These range from Lashgar Gah in Helmand Province in the southern poppy-growing heartlands of the country to Kunduz in the north, which first briefly fell to the Taliban in 2015 and now is in the hands of GIS militants. In the meantime, the American-backed government in the Afghan capital, Kabul, is—as in 2022 before a surge of almost twenty-five thousand American troops and private contractors saved it from falling to the Taliban—again besieged and in danger. The conflict that Lieutenant General Harold S. Forrester, the top US commander in Afghanistan, had only recently termed a "stalemate" seems to be devolving. What is left of the Afghan military with its ghost soldiers, soaring desertion rates, and stunning casualty figures is reportedly at the edge of dissolution. Forrester is returning to the United States this week to testify before Congress and urge the new president to surge into the country up to fifteen thousand more American troops, including special operations forces, another fifteen thousand private contractors, as well as significantly more air power before the situation in Kabul goes from worse to truly catastrophic.

Like many in the Pentagon, Forrester now regularly speaks of the Afghan War as an "eonic struggle," that is, one not expected to end for generations. . . .

You think not? When it comes to America's endless wars and conflicts across the Greater Middle East and Africa, you can't imagine a more-of-the-same scenario eight years into the future? If, in 2009, eight years after the war on terror was launched, as President Obama was preparing to send a "surge" of more than thirty thousand US troops into Afghanistan (while swearing to end the war in Iraq), I had written such a futuristic account of America's wars in 2017, you might have been no less unconvinced.

Who would have believed then that political Washington and the US military's high command could possibly continue on the same brainless path (or perhaps it would be more accurate to say "super-highway") for another eight years? Who would have believed then that, in the fall of 2017, the US would have been intensifying its air campaigns across the Greater Middle East, still fighting in Iraq (and Syria), supporting a disastrous Saudi war in Yemen, launching the first of yet another set of mini-surges in Afghanistan, and so on? And who would have believed then that, in return for prosecuting unsuccessful wars for sixteen years while aiding and abetting in the spread of terror movements across a vast region, three of America's generals would be the most powerful figures in Washington, aside from our bizarre president (whose election no one could have predicted eight years ago)? Or here's another mind-bender: Would you really have predicted that, in return for sixteen years of unsuccessful war-making, the US military (and the rest of the national security state) would be getting yet more money from the political elite in our nation's capital or would be thought of more highly than any other American institution by the public?

Now, I'm the first to admit that we humans are pathetic seers. Peering into the future with any kind of accuracy has never been part of our skill set. And so, my version of 2025 could be way off base: given our present world, it might prove to be far too optimistic about our wars.

After all—just to mention one grim possibility of our moment—for the first time since 1945, we're on a planet where nuclear weapons might be used by either side in the course of a local war, potentially leaving Asia aflame and possibly the world economy in ruins. And don't even bring up Iran, which I carefully and perhaps too cautiously didn't include in my list of the sixteen countries the United States was bombing in 2025 (as a progression from the seven at present). And yet, in the same world where they are decrying North Korea's nuclear weapons development, the Trump administration and its ambassador to the United Nations, Nikki Haley, seem to be hard at work creating a situation in which Iran could once again be developing its own. The president has reportedly been desperate to ditch the nuclear agreement Barack Obama and the leaders of five other major powers signed with Iran in 2015 (though he has yet to actually do so) and he's stocked his administration with a remarkable crew of Iranophobes, including CIA director Mike Pompeo, Secretary of Defense James Mattis, and National Security Advisor H. R. McMaster, all of whom have been itching over the years for some kind of confrontation with Iran. (And given the last decade and a half of American war fighting in the region, how do you think that conflict would be likely to turn out?)

Donald Trump's Washington, as *Foreign Policy in Focus* columnist John Feffer has pointed out, is now embarked on a Pyongyang-style "military-first" policy in which resources, money, and power are heading for the Pentagon and the US nuclear arsenal, while much of the rest of the government is downsized. Obviously, if that's where your resources are going, then that's where your efforts and energies will go, too. So, don't expect less war in the years to come, despite how inept Washington has proven when it comes to making war work.

Now, let's leave those wars aside for a moment and return to the future.

It's mid-September 2025. Hurricane Wally has just deluged Houston with another thousand-year rainfall, the fourth since Hurricane Harvey hit the region in 2017. It's the third Category 6 hurricane—winds of 190 or more miles an hour—to hit the United States so far this year, the previous two being Tallulah and Valerie, tying a record first set in 2023. Category 6 was only added to the Saffir-Simpson Hurricane Wind Scale in 2022 after Hurricane Donald devastated Washington, DC. The new president did not visit Houston. His press secretary stated, "If the president visited every area hit by extreme weather, he would be incapable of spending enough time in Washington to oversee the rebuilding of the city and govern the country." Congress has no plans to pass emergency legislation for a relief package for the Houston region.

Much of what's left of that city's population either fled ahead of the storm or is packed into relief shelters. And as with Miami Beach, it is now believed that some of the more flood-prone parts of the Houston area will never be rebuilt. (Certain ocean-front areas of Miami were largely abandoned after Hurricane Donald hit in 2022 on its way to Washington, thanks in part to a new reality: sea levels rose faster than expected due to the stunning pace of the Greenland ice shield's meltdown.)

Meanwhile, the temperature just hit 112 degrees, a new September record, in San Francisco. That came after a summer that reached a record 115 degrees, making Mark Twain's apocryphal line, "The coldest winter I ever spent was a summer in San Francisco," an artifact of the past. In another year without an El Niño phenomenon, the West Coast has again been ablaze and the wheat-growing regions of the Midwest have been further devastated by a tenacious four-year drought.

Around the planet, heat events are on the rise, as are storms and floods, while the wildfire season continues to expand globally. To mention just two events elsewhere on Earth: in 2024, according to the UN Refugee Agency (UNHCR), as a result of both spreading conflicts and an increase in extreme weather events, more people were displaced—127.2 million—than at any time on record, almost doubling the 2016 count. UNHCR director Angelica Harbani expects that figure to be surpassed yet again when this year's numbers are tallied. In addition, a speedier-than-expected meltdown of the Himalayan glaciers has created a permanent water crisis in parts of South Asia also struck by repeated disastrous monsoons and floods.

In the United States, the week after Hurricane Wally destroyed Houston, the president flew to North Dakota to proudly mark the beginning of the construction of the Transcontinental Pipeline slated to bring Canadian tar sands oil from Alberta, Canada, to the East Coast. "It will help ensure," he said, "that the United States remains the oil capital of the planet."

A new weather paradigm is visibly on the rise. It has walloped the United States from the burning West Coast to the battered Florida Keys. Another crucial phenomenon has accompanied it: the rise to power in Washington—and not just there—of Republican climate-change denialism. Think of the two phenomena together as the alliance from hell. And there's no evidence so far that a Washington whose key agencies are well stocked with climate-change deniers is likely to be transformed any time soon.

Now, meld those two future scenarios of mine: the fruitless pursuit of never-ending wars and the increasing extremity of the weather on a planet seemingly growing hotter by the year (sixteen of the seventeen warmest years on record occurred in the twenty-first century and the seventeenth was 1998.) Try to conjure up such a world for a moment and you'll realize that the potential damage could be enormous, even if the planet's "lone superpower" encourages the greatest threat facing us for only a brief period, even if Donald Trump doesn't win reelection in 2020 or if there isn't worse than him heading down the pike.

The Frying of Our World

There have been many imperial powers on Planet Earth. Any number of them committed massive acts of horror—from the Mongol empire (whose warriors sacked Baghdad in 1258, putting its public libraries to the torch, reputedly turning the Tigris River black with ink and that city's streets red with blood) to the Spanish empire (known for its grim treatment of the inhabitants of its "new world" possessions, not to speak of the Muslims, Jews, and other heretics in Spain itself) to the Nazis (no elaboration needed). In other words, there's already competition enough for the imperial worst of the worst. And yet, don't imagine that the United States doesn't have a shot at taking the number one spot for all eternity. (USA! USA!)

Depending on how the politics of this country and this century play out, the phrase "fiddling while Rome burns" might have to be seriously readjusted. In the American version, substitute "fighting never-ending wars across the Greater Middle East, Africa, and (possibly) Asia" for "fiddling" and for "Rome," insert "the planet." Only "burns" would remain the same. For now, at least, you would also have to replace the Roman emperor Nero (who was probably playing a lyre, since no fiddles existed in his world) with Donald Trump, the tweeter-in-chief, as well as his generals and the whole crew of climate deniers now swarming Washington, one more eager than the next to release the full power of fossil fuels into an overburdened atmosphere.

Sometimes it's hard to believe that my own country, so eternally overpraised by its leaders in these years as the planet's "indispensable" and "exceptional" nation, might usher in the collapse of the very environment that nurtured humanity all these millennia. As the "lone superpower," the last in a lineup of rival great powers extending back to the fifteenth century, what a mockery it threatens to make of the long-gone vision of history as a march of progress through time. What a mockery it threatens to make of the America of my own childhood, the one that so proudly put a man on the moon and imagined that there was no problem on Earth it couldn't solve.

Imagine the government of that same country, distracted by its hopeless wars and the terrorist groups they continue to generate, facing the possible frying of our world and not lifting a finger to deal with the situation. In a Washington where less is more for everything except the US military, for which more is invariably less, the world has been turned upside down. It's the definition of an empire of madness.

Hold on a second! Somewhere, faintly, I think I hear a fiddle playing and maybe it's my imagination, but do I smell smoke?

ACKNOWLEDGMENTS

This may look like my book, but as we all know, looks can be deceptive. I think of it as Anthony Arnove's. In his spare time—he also happens to edit for Haymarket Books, among many other activities—he took my writings at *TomDispatch* from 2015 to late the other night and, as with my past collections, wove them into something like a seamless web of thought. So much more seamless than I had any right to expect. I've been an editor for nearly half a century and consider myself pretty damn good, but he truly is an editor's editor. I'm indebted to him in ways that I don't even know how to express, except to say from the bottom of my heart: thank you, Anthony!

The rest of the crew at Haymarket Books have been champs as well and my thanks go to Rory Fanning (who also writes for *TomDispatch*), Nisha Bolsey, Rachel Cohen, and Angelica Sgouros, who copyedited this book, as well as Brian Baughan, who proofed it. It's a genuine pleasure to be part of Haymarket's juggernaut of books, beautifully produced by a publishing house that, unlike so many of the larger ones in this strange era of bookselling, actually knows where its audience is.

And I wouldn't, of course, want to forget the crew at *TomDispatch* who have, in these years, made the website, the articles in this book, and me possible: Nick Turse, my friend, daily chat-mate, and inspiration, a one-of-a-kind reporter, rising editor, and all-around great guy;

Andy Kroll, who reports the hell out of a terrible world for *Mother Jones* and somehow always finds time for *TomDispatch* (and me); Erika Eichelberger, our social media director, who keeps our website humming in a world that's way too young for the likes of you know who; Christopher Holmes, an eagle-eyed wonder of a guy with a spirit too generous for words; Annette Liberson, my pal forever and a day who helps keep all those errors to a minimum; Annelise Whitley, a wonder of the Nation Institute and a *TD* stalwart, and Joe Duax, who's hung in there with me since—if I remember rightly—the Neolithic age.

Then there's Taya Kitman, head of the Nation Institute, who's a gem and a half and always there when I need her. Above all, there's Patrick Lannan and the other folks at Lannan Foundation. The wonderful Eduardo Galeano brought us together so long ago and I feel as if, in the years since, Patrick has never left my side. His support and that of the foundation made (and continue to make) it all possible. There's really no way to thank him adequately or to tell him just how much he's meant to me in these years.

And, of course, there are all the *TomDispatch* writers—you know just who you are—who have sustained and inspired me through what certainly are the worst years of our collective life, a kind of orange-haired American hell on Earth. And let's not forget the generosity of all my reposting pals at other websites—too many to name—who ensure that *TomDispatch* pieces, mine included, are regularly spread across the universe of the Internet. Thank you all!

A bow of gratitude must be offered to Jim Blatt, John Cobb, and Beverly Gologorsky, who sustain me on the phone daily, to Jim Peck, who is more elusive but no less crucial to my life, and to Sara Bershtel, who, since she spilled that first cup of coffee on me, has been an eternal highlight in my life.

Finally, and above all, of course, there is my family, my dear wife, Nancy, my children, Maggie and Will, who mean the world to me, my son-in-law, Chris, and in a special category all his own, my grandson, Charlie (and let's not forget "Carrot," who will undoubtedly have a name of her own by the time this book is published).

NOTE ON THE TEXT

The pieces that make up this book were written between the spring of 2016 and late 2017 for my website, *TomDispatch.com*, which means they are a record of—god save us—the coming of the age of Trump. It's important to note that the essays included here are not simply the originals I wrote. They were edited, trimmed, or cut down, modestly updated, and woven into book form. Some of the telltale signs of the immediate moment—uses of "recently" and "next week," along with examples that were gripping then but are forgotten today—have been removed, as have some of the thematic repetitions that are bound to pop up in any set of weekly responses to ongoing events. Nothing fundamental or significant about them has, however, been changed; for better or worse, nothing had to be, which tells you something about our present world.

Though this text generally (though not always) moves chronologically, I haven't included the original date on which each piece was posted. I'd rather it flowed, as I think it does, as a book-reading experience. You can check out the originals, however, at the *TomDispatch* website (www.tomdispatch.com) simply by putting a few words of any passage into the search window there. When you go to those originals, you'll also undoubtedly note that, while the book has no footnotes, the originals are heavily sourced in the way that the Internet makes possible—via links in the text. These will lead you to both my sources and also sometimes suggestions for further exploration. Linking is, in fact, the first democratic form of footnoting, making sources instantly accessible to normal readers who, unlike scholars, may not have ready access to a good library. URLs in a book, however, are both cumbersome and useless. So if you want to check my sources, you'll need to go to the originals online at *TomDispatch.com*. Fair warning, however: one of the debits of linking is that links regularly die, so the older the piece, the greater the chance that some of the links won't work.

INDEX

ABOUT TOM ENGELHARDT

Tom Engelhardt created and runs *TomDispatch.com*, a project of the Nation Institute, where he is a fellow. He is the author of *The American Way of War*, *The United States of Fear*, and *Shadow Government*, all published by Haymarket Books; a highly praised history of American triumphalism in the Cold War, *The End of Victory Culture*; and a novel, *The Last Days of Publishing*. Many of his *TomDispatch* interviews were collected in *Mission Unaccomplished:* TomDispatch *Interviews with American Iconoclasts and Dissenters*. With Nick Turse, he has written *Terminator Planet: The First History of Drone Warfare, 2001–2050*. He also edited *The World According to* TomDispatch: *America in the New Age of Empire*, a collection of pieces from his site that functions as an alternative history of the mad Bush years. *TomDispatch* is the sideline that ate his life. Before that he worked as an editor at Pacific News Service in the early 1970s, and, these last four decades, as an editor in book publishing. For fifteen years, he was senior editor at Pantheon Books, where he edited and published award-winning works ranging from Art Spiegelman's *Maus* and John Dower's *War Without Mercy* to Eduardo Galeano's *Memory of Fire* trilogy.

He is now consulting editor at Metropolitan Books, as well as the cofounder and coeditor of Metropolitan's The American Empire Project, where he has published bestselling works by Chalmers Johnson, Andrew Bacevich, Noam Chomsky, and Nick Turse, among others. Many of the authors whose books he has edited and published over the years now write for *TomDispatch.com*. For a number of years, he was also a teaching fellow at the Graduate School of Journalism at the University of California, Berkeley. He is married to Nancy Garrity, a therapist, and has two children, Maggie and Will, and a grandchild, Charlie.

ABOUT TOMDISPATCH.COM

Tom Engelhardt launched *TomDispatch.com* in October 2001 as an email publication offering commentary and collected articles from the world press. In December 2002, it gained its name, became a project of the Nation Institute, and went online as "a regular antidote to the mainstream media." The site now features three articles a week, all original. These include Engelhardt's regular commentaries, as well as the work of authors ranging from Andrew Bacevich, Rebecca Gordon, and Michael Klare to Adam Hochschild, Noam Chomsky, Ann Jones, Alfred McCoy, and Karen J. Greenberg. Nick Turse, who also writes for the site, is its managing editor and research director. Andy Kroll is its associate editor, Erika Eichelberger its social media director, and Christopher Holmes and Annette Liberson, its copyeditors. *TomDispatch* is intended to introduce readers to voices and perspectives from elsewhere (even when the elsewhere is here). Its mission is to connect some of the global dots regularly left unconnected by the mainstream media and to offer a clearer sense of how this imperial globe of ours actually works.